# QUIET THE NOISE

## VOLUME 2

# QUIET THE NOISE

## VOLUME 2

## Trail Running, Hearing God and Achieving "Impossible" Goals!

# Rami F. Odeh, MS

*Quiet The Noise, Volume 2*
Title ID - 7054724
Copyright © 2015 by Rami F. Odeh, MS. All rights reserved.

This book is designed to provide accurate and authoritative information with regard to the subject matter covered. This information is given with the understanding that the author is not engaged in rendering legal, professional advice. Since the details of your situation are fact dependent, you should additionally seek the services of a competent professional.

Published by Deep Stillness Publishing
(A wholly owned subsidiary of Quiet the Noise, LLC)

Published in the United States of America

EAN-13 - 9781545061671

1. Sports & Recreation / Running & Jogging
2. Biography & Autobiography / Personal Memoirs
15.04.27

This book, and everything I am and do, is dedicated to the glory of the Father, the Son, and the Holy Spirit.

From whom we receive everything we have, do, and are.

Without whom, nothing at all is possible.

It is also dedicated to my wonderful family—Heather, Ryan, and Hana.

# Contents

# PART 1
# NOW WHAT?

*Let all men know that grace comes after tribulation.*
*Let them know that without the burden of afflictions*
*it is impossible to reach the height of grace. Let them*
*know that the gifts of grace increase as the struggles*
*increase. Let men take care not to stray or to be*
*deceived. This is the only true ladder to paradise, and*
*without the cross, there is no other way in which to*
*ascend to heaven.*

—Our Lord to St. Rose of Lima

# A Different Way to Hear God

*He gives power to the faint, abundant strength to the*
*weak. Though young men faint and grow weary, and*
*youths stagger and fall, they that hope in the* Lord
*will renew their strength, they will soar on eagles'*
*wings; They will run and not grow weary, walk and*
*not grow faint.*

—Isaiah 40:29–31 (NAB)

This might seem like a strange way to continue a series of books on how trail running can help you hear God, but bear with me!

While I was training for my fifty-three-mile trail running race (the completion of my first book), I did a caving (actual spelunking, not a cave tour) expedition with the Cub Scout troop my son, Ryan, was in.

It was amazingly difficult and fun (for us anyway, about 25 percent of the dads dropped out after the first belly crawl), and Ryan had been asking me to take him back (just the two of us) for a year afterward.

So I promised him we would do it for his tenth birthday.

Ryan really loves this stuff, and I do too.

However, probably not quite as much as him.

It helps that he is a lean, strong, and extremely flexible young man and I am a fairly strong, two-hundred-pound, not-flexible-at–all, not-so-young man. As you can guess, in most of the challenges, especially those crawling through small holes, he is way better than me!

Here's a side note of God's wonderful interventions:

1. We were originally talking about bringing a friend of mine and his son, and we both decided we could not wait till they were available and went on our own.

   Well, it turns out that it was so dangerous and challenging that he (my friend is a radiologist and even less flexible than me) would probably have dropped out or hated it.

   On top of that, his son is very athletic but tends to get really stressed out in challenging situations and pukes a lot.

   Not a good mix in this cave.

2. Going alone allowed us the luxury of it being just the two of us and the guide (which actually made me a little apprehensive at first).

3. Finally, it turns out that the weekend after we went was their busiest weekend of the year, so we would have been in a large group; the stars were aligned, as they say.

Truth be told, I felt that God was rewarding me, honoring my role as a father—to support my son in things like this that will help to make him a man—and making me a better man!

Anyway, back to our trip. We packed up and left Atlanta about 3:00 p.m. to head for Tennessee (about a two-hour drive). I love driving anywhere with my son. It is awesome and very laid-back. He has very little demands, and we both sort of zone out into whatever we are doing. Sometimes, there's lots of conversation, sometimes none, and it's all good.

We arrived about one hour early, so we had a very light dinner (you cannot eat or drink anything the whole time you are in the cave, and you don't want to have to go to the bathroom) and headed to the cave site. We met our guide—a very cool and laid-back guy named Matt—and headed into the cave.

Immediately, we could tell this would be different than the Cub Scout trip, just in the pacing. Without having to wait for thirty kids and dads, we could really rock this trip, not so fast that we missed anything, but just the right pace. Also—and the guide told us this—with two people in decent shape, he could take us off the beaten path into areas that none of the "normal" people go on.

Without going into a huge amount of detail—'cause that is not what this chapter is about—this ended up being one of the most challenging and definitely the scariest two hours of my life, and *I loved* it (Ryan loved it even more than me, if that was possible). Notice I said two hours. We covered more area of the cave, much harder routes, in two hours and fifteen minutes than we did in over four hours with the Scouts!

By the way, this is no Disney ride where you are scared but you know how safe it is and that you are strapped in. You are literally one step (a very muddy, slippery step), away from falling into a crevasse and breaking a leg, at the very least.

You are leaning over and putting your body weight on your hands, with your feet on a small ledge, above a thirty-foot drop into sharp rocks!

You are crawling through holes that touch you on all points of your body. I got stuck more than once and had to readjust to make it through.

To say this is exhilarating would be an understatement.

Now before you go judging me as a reckless and uncaring dad, remember, my son is very, very capable—at some points, he actually got ahead of the guide, and we had to pull him back—and the guide was giving us instruction as needed.

He really is an amazing kid, very resilient and up for any challenge that comes his way. He likes to say, "Let's do this thing!" We had an ongoing joke that the guide would say, over and over, "Okay, now comes the hard part," and we would laugh. Didn't he just say that five minutes ago?

Another very cool observation is that every time we would get to a crossroad, the guide would give us a choice, and Ryan would ask, "Which way is harder?"

Of course, that was the way we would go!

What ten-year-old does that? I actually was talking to the guide about the book *The Road Less Traveled* , and we both said Ryan has that concept down, which is a great thing, at least in these type of situations!

I was so proud of my boy!

Here is the takeaway from this weekend. For two hours (really for almost twenty-four if you include the euphoric stage after we were done), I thought of nothing, and I mean *nothing*, except where to put my hands, how to make it through a squeeze, and how to turn my body around and slide down a ledge. All the while, I was keeping my eye on Ryan to see if he needed my help (not much) and making sure we were both safe.

I didn't think about work, about my challenging marriage, about our financial situation, about the current political situation, etc.

Nothing but the moment.

It was absolutely amazing, similar to what I felt during my first triathlon, but with the added danger factor and excitement of doing something totally out of my athletic box.

Side note to self: try rock climbing and mountain climbing as a new adventure soon!

After we were done, we both said that this was in the top ten experiences of our lives!

Seriously.

A big deal for a ten-year-old but a really big deal for a forty-nine-year-old who had done a fair amount in his life!

We enjoyed the longest, best hot shower in recent memory and then tried to sleep in the cave. In retrospect, this is one of only two things I would change. I'd wear a long sleeve T-shirt 'cause my arms got pretty trashed and either camp out if the weather is good or get a hotel. Sleeping on rock is just impossible for a two-hundred-pound man, even with a good mattress; you wake up every twenty minutes for the whole night!

The upside is that it makes you appreciate your home and bed so much more!

By the way, caving (like we did it) burns about five hundred calories per hour, and we ate hardly anything, so we were starving, and I mean hand-shaking starving, the morning after—amazing!

I was so peaceful the day after and thankful that we were alive and safe.

I felt like I could take on anything the next week brought me.

God cleared my noisy brain again, and I am thankful for it!

The next time you are scared to do something physical, I hope you can remember this chapter and realize what is awaiting you on the other side of that challenge—peace.

## *Summer 2011*

The summer of 2011 was pretty uneventful as far as epic, life-changing, noise-quieting, and hearing-God training runs and races went.

In an effort to shake this up, I decided to do a training weekend at the marathon course I would be running on October 9, 2011 . I have run this course—the Mystery Mountain Marathon—three times, the first time as the twelve-mile option and two more times as the full marathon.

All three times have inspired chapters in my books, mostly because of the difficulty and beauty of this course and what finishing this thing brings out of me physically, emotionally, and spiritually!

The RD (race director or, as she likes to be called, MFO or most fabulous one) set up a training weekend where you basically did the easy first twelve miles on Saturday, camped out, and then did the not-so-easy sixteen miles Sunday (I know, this adds up to more than 26.2 miles, but that is the way us ultra people roll. Everything is measured in -ish terms).

I headed up around lunchtime on Saturday, as the run started at 2:00 p.m.—yes, 2:00 p.m. in August. We would be running about three hours. Needless to say, I was not looking forward to this. Luckily, we were blessed as Hurricane Irene brought in some cooler temps and lower humidity, so even though it was ninety-two degrees, it was not nearly as bad as it could have been.

We really took it easy, and it still beat me down pretty badly. I am just *not* a heat runner. We finished in just under three hours, which may sound really slow—well, it was really slow.

However, this course has been measured by some (remember, *-ish*) to have fifteen thousand feet of elevation change over twenty-six (twenty-eight?) miles. Basically, we go up and down a 2,600-foot mountain six times!

Not for the faint of heart, especially the downhills!

After we were done, we set up camp, had an adult beverage or two, and headed into the local town for Mexican food (I know, what kind of camping trip is this?). It was really fun and great to break bread with fifteen others who completely understand why I do this stuff. I think the coolest part of the evening was my buddy, whom I'd brought with me, noting that he had "never seen such a happy group of people. You are all high on endorphins 24/7!" This is so true.

After dinner, we had a nice fire, made s'mores, had a few more adult beverages, and hit the sack around 10:00 p.m. I did not sleep well at all—not sure why—and ended up waking up at 6:00 a.m. after about two hours of sleep, wondering how the heck I was going to complete four hours of running on the hardest section of the course! Also, this section has a 3.5- to 4-mile uphill section (that falls from mile 18–22 in the marathon) that has kicked my butt in previous years, so I really wanted to show it who was boss this day, mostly to build confidence for the race.

Long story short, somehow, I had one of the best runs I have had in months. I felt strong all day; I finished sixteen miles in three hours and forty-five minutes and could have kept running! I am convinced it had to do with the awesome high-fat meal I had the night before—chicken, avocado, onions, and something called Mexican sausage. I know, this was a risk, but call me a wild man. I like to live on the edge!

Met some great people, learned how to rely on others for directions, learned that ultra runners make great after-race treats (one guy brought homemade cannoli; are you kidding me?), learned (once again) that I enjoy training with others, but I really *love* the solitude of training on my own and having my own schedule, agenda, pacing, etc. Next year, I will go up Friday night and camp out solo. I will do the run early Saturday morning and really relax on Saturday, instead of rushing around like we did this time.

To end on a scary and then good note, when we were heading back to camp to break down our site, a family that camped with us was heading out and said they had just chased a baby bear out of their tent! Could have been a bad scene if momma was around, but all ended well.

I ate about 2,000 calories on the way home, and my quads were sore for a week. I can't wait to do it again!

A common theme/lesson was reinforced this weekend regarding my connection to God when I train or race. While training with others teaches me valuable lessons regarding fellowship, helping others, relying on help from others, etc. the most valuable lessons I learn are not in groups.

They are, and continue to be, learned when I am alone.

## *Burn Out and Barfing*

In this chapter, I will begin by saying that as much as I love running, even I need a break sometimes! At this point in my ultra career, I had hit the wall, burned out, lost motivation, overtrained—you name it, I did it.

After I finished the fifty-three miler, I almost immediately decided to do my first one hundred miler in November of 2011.

I know. Perfect progression, right?

Age 15–Hobble around a fourth of a mile around my block

5K- Well, I actually skipped this one.

Age 18–10K (my first running race)

Age 28–Half marathon (college slowed the progression)

Age 30–Marathon

(Insert fifteen years of multisport events; I lost track of how many after 150.)

Age 47–50K (fifteen years of triathlon racing slowed running progression)

Age 48–40 miler

Age 49–53 miler

Age unknown- 100 miler

Again, you know by now I am not a very intelligent individual!

I put together a training program and then life happened, and I decided it was just not the year to do it.

So I trained with a couple of buddies who were training for the Lake Tahoe fifty miler (kudos to both of them; they both finished 50 miles at altitude—nice!) and then decided to really kick ass in the Mystery Mountain Marathon in October, which has kicked my ass every year.

Well, what this messed up and nondirectional training schedule did was not give me any real recovery time (mostly, what I needed was mental, not physical) after the fifty-three miler, and it had me doing long training all through the summer, my least favorite time of year to train.

About a month before the race, I did a really strong training weekend on the course and felt awesome on the second day (looking back, this is what happens to me a lot when I overtrain—the candle burns brightest; see last chapter) and after that, I lost *all* motivation.

About three weeks before the race, after all my training, I decided to drop down to the twelve-mile option and felt totally fine about it!

It ended up being a great decision. It was a blast to actually run the whole race, as opposed to fast walking the hills and suffering for six hours.

Funny side story, we broke down about three miles from the race and had to hitch a ride to the start; we got to the starting line at 7:52 a.m. for the 8:00 a.m. start!

Since I was doing the twelve, I was fine, but if I was stressing about prepping for a full-on assault at the marathon distance, I would have been *freaking out*!

We make plans, and God laughs.

After that race, I actually stopped logging my training and decided to just free flow until the bug hit me again (didn't take long, BTW).

I was doing sporadic runs—no trail runs over sixty minutes—and starting to do some strength training workouts to get ready for Pinhoti 100 in 2012.

Yep, you read that correctly.

I was able to transfer my entry so unless life got in the way big-time again, I was hitting that starting line and, God willing, finish line in November of 2012!

Okay, so that is the burn out part. Now, what am I talking about with barfing?

Suffice it to say, sometimes, I am not a very good dad.

Let me explain (mistakes or lessons in *italics*).

A old buddy of mine lives down in Miami and does triathlon coaching and sports marketing, and he told me about a trail race that was happening over the Thanksgiving weekend, and guess what, we were going down for the holiday to see family—perfect!

Ryan (my son) and I had been talking about him doing his first trail race (a 10K) on December 3 here in Georgia, and this race had a 5K option, so I thought that might be a better idea (in hindsight, I am *so* glad we didn't sign up for the 10K).

We had about three weeks to train for it, but Ryan is in good shape, and how hard can a trail race in Miami be (it's dead flat, after all)?

*Mistake (lesson) number 1: Because they don't have hills, they designed a mountain bike trail that was so technical that it was like an obstacle course! To add to this, in typical trail running fashion, the 5K turned out to be more like four miles. The 5K winner went twenty-eight minutes, and the 10K winner went fifty-one minutes!*

So we were both severely undertrained.

To add to that, Ryan had been sick, and I hurt my back (worst ever in my life, could hardly walk) in a workout I had no business doing.

My wife commented, "Ryan is sick and won't tell you, and you can hardly walk, and you won't tell him. You both don't want to disappoint each other by not doing the race. Men!"

I won't count this as a mistake, more of a severe character flaw that I have and seem to have passed on to my son, something that is not gonna change.

So we get up at 6:00 a.m. on Sunday for a 7:30 a.m. start; it was all good. I give Ryan a banana and a G2 on the way

*Mistake (lesson) number 2: Ryan was not feeling good and does not have my digestive system. Next time, just sip on water and G2, and if he gets hungry, give him a gel during the race!*

We arrived a bit late and didn't have time to warm up, but that should not have been a problem.

Now digress a bit here before we move on to lesson number 3. When Ry and I train together, he normally asks to go out front 'cause I run too fast when I lead. Then he immediately picks up the pace to a drop-dead sprint! I coached him many times that the race would begin fast and to run his own pace.

*Mistake (lesson) number 3: Don't let a ten-year-old set the beginning pace of a race!*

So the race starts, and Ryan takes off with the lead group!

I'm pretty sure we ran the first mile in under eight minutes, which is *way* faster than *either* of us had any business doing.

We were both caught up in the moment and continued on at this pace for another half mile or so.

Then Ryan starts to slow down—a lot. I mean, almost to a walk.

"What's up, son?"

"Dad, I am getting that throw-uppy feeling."

"Dad, can we walk a bit?"

Uh-oh.

On mile 1.5, we pull off the trail, and he pukes his brains out.

To add insult to injury, there was *absolutely* no privacy on this trail, so everyone we went out ahead of in the beginning passed right by us and saw him puking!

As you can imagine, I am feeling like a pretty bad dad now.

I am also silently wondering how I am going to carry this boy back to the start. Remember, my back is hurting so bad I can hardly run!

Miraculously, he recovered a bit, walked about a half mile, and then started running again.

When we got to the two-mile rest stop and the guy told me we had at least two miles to go (remember, -ish on 3.1-mile distance), I made sure Ryan didn't hear it!

At one point, he said, "Dad, you have said, 'We are almost there,' a few times. I don't think I believe you anymore." Smart boy.

Gotta tell you, as many "lessons" as we experienced that morning, I have rarely been so proud of my boy as when he finished that race!

I told him it took me years to figure out nutrition and pacing and that I *still* make mistakes, so he should not worry about it.

He didn't. He felt really good about himself, good enough to ask to get pizza at 9:00 a.m. and good enough to sign up for another race!

God was with us the whole time, teaching us, guiding us, and protecting us.

We are listening. Thank you so much for the lessons!

Remember, no matter how you feel, we are *all* truly blessed. When you can be thankful for your life every day, even when things seem to suck, you have found true happiness!

## *Injury*

As I mentioned in the last chapter, I hurt my back doing a workout I really had no business doing (just goes to show you that even us "experts" make some major mistakes sometimes).

After my trip to Miami and my run with Ryan, it really was not getting any better. I went to my chiropractor or applied kinesiologist and had him take a look. He diagnosed it and did some minor adjustments/trigger points and stretches.

I felt better immediately and, of course, proceeded to do a forty-minute trail run.

I felt fine after that and did ninety minutes with buddies two days later.

Again, I felt fine during and after the run.

Got up Sunday, went to the gym, and did a very, very light bike spin. I got down on the floor to stretch, and when I went to get up, the pain came back—the worst I have *ever* felt!

It hurt so bad I left the mat and towel I was using on the floor 'cause I couldn't imagine bending down to get them. Had to have my family take my shoes off when I got home! If you have been there, you know the feeling!

Now just to give you some history, I have had back problems ever since I started doing triathlons (1992) but I have managed them pretty well with stretching, strengthening, etc., and recently, once I adopted regular foam roller use, my back has been as good as it has ever been.

I have had it go out many times over the past twenty years, 90 percent of the time when I am tapering for a race. Inactivity is normally the worst thing for my back, but this was beyond anything I had ever felt.

I went back to the chiropractor, got some relief again, and decided to take some time off running (per his instructions). I still did some minor workouts; however, things just were not progressing.

We were now coming up on three weeks into this stupid thing!

Finally, I went in again, and he suggested I take a complete week off from all types of exercise.

Yikes!

I found myself bargaining. "What about yoga, swimming, maybe just stretching?"

He said, "No, do nothing for a week and let's see what happens."

Nothing? Like *nothing*?

Wow, can this addict do it? The pain was severe enough (1,200 mg of Advil a day just to make it to work) that I was willing to try anything.

I did it.

Two weeks of no running and almost one week without any other type of exercise! Might not sound like a lot, but if you have been following along, you know that this is way, way out of my box.

What have I learned?

- This injury was the first one in my life that actually responded better to inactivity than light or modified activity. I still feel, based on my thirty-five years of personal experience and twenty years of experience training clients that 95 percent of injuries do better with light activity than total rest, but when the pain is this bad, sometimes ya gotta just lay off, especially when you have been training as long and hard as I have!

- Total inactivity can actually be fun and relaxing for me—for about two to three days. Then it just plain sucks. At first, my energy levels soared. I slept well and felt very calm and peaceful (a very strong sign my body needed the downtime). After about three days, the lethargy and malaise set in. I cannot imagine how anyone can live like that!

- My spiritual life is really helping my chronic anxiety! Normally, I need morning exercise like an addict needs their fix to calm me down and help me face the day peacefully. During this process, my mood was fine and anxiety very low, even with no exercise at all. Praise God!

- The quality of my diet is directly correlated with how much I am training. When I don't train, my diet just plain sucks, kind of like having a race car that just sits in the garage (okay, maybe I am not a race car, but how about a really fast VW bug?). Why bother spending any money on expensive, high quality gas for it? Cookies and ice cream are my new best friends. I was not totally out of control, so I kept my weight gain to about three pounds, mostly water weight.

- I really enjoy running and miss it (this was not a revelation at all, just a nice affirmation). I don't miss weight training as much (more like, I miss the feeling *after* a really tough weight training workout than the process itself), but I really could not wait to get back out on those trails!

- There is a lot more time in your day when you don't train; however, since I am not as sharp or motivated, the extra time I have really does not add up to any more productivity or quality time with my friends and family—another fact I already knew and preach all the time, but it was good to see it in action firsthand.

- Health is a complete blessing that we should never, ever take for granted. I have always felt this way, but times like this just push that point home even stronger!

The good news is that my back got better. Not perfect—it probably never will be—but better. And for that, I thank God.

## *No Pressure*

In 2011, I decided to sign up for my first "Fat Ass" ultra run (a 50K). These are basically grassroots runs—no entry fee, no T-shirt, no prizes. People bring their own aid station water and food and share.

It's really an organized group run. People sometimes keep track of the finishers and sometimes don't.

I had signed up before I decided to postpone my 100 miler and was planning on doing the whole 50K as it would be some good training, and it was held on one of my favorite trails.

Red Top Mountain is a beautiful single track—not too technical, not very hilly, and covered with pine needles almost the whole way!

Since I was not doing the 100 miler, I decided still to go to see what it was like and run as far as I felt like. I stayed up late the night before, had a few drinks, and slept about three hours before the alarm went off. The "race" (with a few friends who were doing the whole 50K) started at 7:00 a.m. The course was a 5.5-mile loop, so we could leave all our stuff at the cars.

Since I was just doing this for training and not having to finish a certain distance based on my goals, the pressure was off, and I could really enjoy the moment much more than normal!

About halfway through the third lap, I started to get that miserable, tired, "not wanting to be here" feeling I get when I am overheated, and I started to think, *How am I going to do this for three more hours, and the suffering is going to be immense, and…wait a minute! I don't have to finish this!*

Immediately, I started to feel better and ran the rest of the lap feeling strong and happy. Those 16.5 miles were more than enough when not training for a major race.

A great group of people, a fun course, and a cold beer at 10:00 a.m. afterward—good stuff!

My plan became to just tag along with others training for big races and keep up my training to a marathon level.

More importantly, the plan was to continue to search out the benefits of having those deep connections with the Lord while, at the same time, staying in shape for future marathons.

At this point, I was making commitments to meet others to train. When training with other runners, I take it seriously and run much longer than I would on my own, but I was also feeling no pressure whatsoever to finish the whole course—the best of both worlds.

# (RELATIVE) SPEED ON TRAILS

*Thus I do not run aimlessly; I do not fight as if I were
shadowboxing. No, I drive my body and train it, for
fear that, after having preached to others, I myself
should be disqualified.*

—1 Corinthians 9:26–27 (NAB)

One of the things that almost everyone encounters when
they first run on the trails, especially in the mountains, is
how different it is from road running, especially regarding
the pacing.

I try to explain to people that this is not like running
on the roads at an eight-minute pace for five hours with no
breaks. It is more like a really slow run, with lots of breaks
and fast walking the hills!

This makes it much more attainable and understandable
for people who have never done it.

Pure road runners hate it and usually never come back.
That is fine with us!

I cannot imagine pounding my body for hours on a
boring road, hot and exposed to traffic. However, hours in
the woods feels like fun, adventure, unplanned excitement
to me! Let me give you a good example of what a trail run
is like.

This run was with a small group. We were all training
for a 30K or 50K in November of that year on the trails we
would be running this day.

The run started at a really nice little park in North
Georgia (Vogel State Park) at 8:00 a.m. I got up there

around 7:30 a.m. to warm up and take care of business before others showed up.

The nine of us got started at about 8:15 a.m. for what was predicted (by Robert, the cruel man who designed this course and the race director for this race) to be a 3–3.5 hour run of about fifteen miles. It ended up being sixteen miles with ten thousand feet of elevation change, and it took me four hours and fifteen minutes. I was the third person done (really the second as one person who beat me back got lost and cut out part of the course)! Here is how the course laid out:

- We went uphill for about a mile right out of the parking lot; it was not tough but not too easy either. There was a very nice trail and great scenery. It was a very cool morning, and everyone started out way too fast in this section, trying to run hills they really had no business running!

- Then came a long, steady, very fun downhill for 2ish miles. I stayed in the back here 'cause I *love* downhills and knew this would be a long day if I trashed my quads three miles into the run!

- At 3.5 miles, we hit the low point of the course—2,100 feet. For the next four miles, we climbed, almost the whole time, up to 4,200 feet! Do the math. This equates to about a 10 percent average incline. We probably fast hiked 90 percent of this section!

- Then, for added cruelty, we dropped (no switchbacks) almost straight down for about .5–1 mile to where the RD had stashed water, Gatorade, and treats (BTW, I saw a guy I know from other runs coming down this hill fully decked out in overnight attire carrying two full gallons of water; I found out later he was out on a twenty-four-hour run!)

- Took me about two hours and fifteen minutes to get here. You get the picture here—over two hours to do eight miles. No seven-minute-per-mile pace on this trip!

- After too long of a break, I couldn't wait any longer and headed back the same way by myself (yep, a four-mile *downhill*. Thank God I do lots of functional leg training that strengthens my quads and ankles!).

Total time running was about four hours and fifteen minutes (I know, sounds slow as s———, but if you look at the website for this trail, and it says average time for twelve miles—we added four—is nine hours, so we were not too shabby). It was an amazing trail, with lots of amazing scenery and cool new people. I ran two hours and fifteen minutes with people and two hours completely solo (interestingly, with no iPod, I ended up singing to myself to scare away bears and to pass the time on the downhills. Another realization was that I don't know all the words to many songs and seem to gravitate toward "Desparado" and "Turn the Page" a lot).

Felt fantastic afterward.

No real mental or spiritual epiphanies on this trip. Just wanted to share what a long trail run is like, at least for me (I am sure there are a few studs out there that would run this whole thing, but not many!).

So join me on my next one. Don't think of it as a run. Think of a fun day hiking, jogging, and meeting new friends in God's nature!

## *Actually Running Again*

In early 2012, I competed (I guess you could call it that) in an 11.5-mile trail race at Red Top Mountain.

This race venue was actually where my second-ever trail race was back in 2008, and it's one of my favorite places to run off-road in Atlanta. If you get a chance to run out there, do not hesitate. There are groomed trails; it's easy to navigate and not that hilly at all.

Well, not hilly when you train there.

Racing? Well, that's a different story.

So this year was a complete question mark to me. I seriously hurt my back in November and had to take a lot of time off. I had only had about four weeks of limited mileage before this race. I was hoping muscle memory would kick in!

Traveled up to the race with two buddies—one old friend (years and years of being my friend) and one new (also had years and years of being my friend).

It was too funny. Two middle-aged dudes in the front seat listening to the typical ranting and stories that a twenty-five-year-old tends to tell. It seemed like every story began with, "So there was this girl," had in the middle, "So, I was drunk," and finished with, "Then, I was so damn hung over, and I had to explain all my drunk calls and text messages."

Felt a bit old, but it was fun to listen to him (on a side note, I beat him by thirteen minutes in the race so that felt pretty good; he is twenty-four years my junior).

I felt really good all morning, especially warming up, so I figured I would take it out hard and see if my body still was able to run. Man, an 8:03 mile hurts like *crazy* when you have been training at a 12-minute-per-mile pace! Somehow, I was able to maintain this pace for the whole flat section, then make up for my ridiculously slow uphill pace. Note to self, gotta work on this before Pinhoti.

With my lack of fear and *huge* body weight, which allows me to make up a ton of time on the downhills, I averaged about 9 minute per miles, which, for where I was then and how much I was training, was a happy moment for me!

It was really cool to be at a race where, four years previously, I knew only one person. Now I had a bunch of new friends there to hang out with after the race. That's the best part of any race, especially trail races!

Here's a side note on consistency or how we tend to gravitate toward a specific pace in racing.

In 2008, I had no idea what to expect and walked a lot of it. I had a great time, felt very easy, and finished in 1:48. Let's not count that race 'cause it doesn't emphasize the crazy consistency I have in racing.

In 2009, I walked all the hills, but with more trail running experience, I ran the downhills and flats hard and finished in 1:44:07.

In 2010, I decided to push the whole race. I never walked once and ended up running 1:44:08. Yes, I didn't walk and *lost* one second; it shows you how much time you lose by going totally anaerobic on the hills and taking too much time to recover on the downhills and flats.

In 2011, I dragged my feet and the race sold out before I could sign up. Bummer!

In 2012, I was undertrained, coming off a major injury. I pushed as hard as I could, walked most of the hills, and ended up finishing in 1:44:09!

At this rate of speed decline, it will take me 51 more years to go over 1:45.

## *Four Miles of Bliss: The Sequel*

If you read my last book, you will remember that my son Ryan and I competed in his first running race in June 2011 at the Father's Day four miler at Braves Stadium. It was totally and completely awesome!

So awesome, in fact, that we decided to do it again in 2012—his first repeat race.

Those of you that are runners, triathletes, etc. know that repeat races are a double-edged sword. On the one hand, you know what to expect, so you can prepare. On the other hand, you know what to expect, and this can cause worry and anxiety!

My son has a very, very good memory (much better than mine—I tend to have a selective memory, especially when it comes to the difficulty of races), and so he remembered that this was not a flat course and that running four miles without walking, hiking, or stopping to look at turtles is *not* easy!

On top of this, we were not able to get in as much training that year as the previous year for various reasons. This added to his (and my) anxiety leading up to race day.

On Friday night, he had to go to bed early like dad because we had a 6:00 a.m. wake-up call. This was not easy as it was summer, and he was consistently staying up till midnight!

Went in to wake him up Saturday morning, and he was tired. He told me he was nervous and couldn't sleep very well. I told him this was a good sign.

Fortunately, we learned our lesson with the barfing incident at his first trail race. Eating a banana and drinking a G2 thirty minutes before the race worked well with my "mature" gut, not so much with his small stomach.

We had him eat a small energy bar at 6:30 a.m. (a full hour before race start) and just sip on a G2 for the next hour. This was *perfect* prerace nutrition for a ten-year-old. BTW, he did great with his stomach, hydration, etc.!

The drive down to the race site was a blast. Ryan is normally the quieter of my two children, especially in the car, but this time, he never, ever stopped talking. At one point, he actually asked, "Do you think I am bit nervous? I am talking a lot!"

I left plenty of time to get to the start and get our numbers—too much time, in fact. I don't think I have ever had so much downtime before a race started. It was fun at first—sparked a cool discussion about the relativity of time—but we were both ready and anxious to get started, so I won't get there so early next time!

As we warmed up, did drills, and stretched, Ryan came up with a little song—"Two-minute run, two-minute run"—not much to it, but it was good foreshadowing for the race, and I think he learned how great it is to have a mantra in a competition!

The race started, and he took off, much slower than his last race (puking after one mile of all-out sprinting taught him a valuable lesson about pacing), and he was still singing, "Two-minute run, two-minute run," and I realize this could be another good teaching opportunity—having a solid mantra and breaking down goals into smaller segments.

So last year, the race took us a little over forty minutes. We estimated that we only had twentyish two-minute runs to the finish. We actually counted them down for a while to help pass the time and help us realize we were getting closer to our goal.

As the race progressed, Ryan got a bit less chatty (hills will do that to you). However, at one point, we were climbing the toughest hill on the course, and we went by two ladies who were slowing down and struggling a bit, and they commented on how strong he looked. He responded with—and I paraphrase—"Thank you. Is this the first time you are doing this race? We did it last year, and it gets easier after this. You guys are doing awesome! Keep it up!" A natural coach/trainer in the making! I just loved that, in the middle of his suffering, he was able to get outside of himself and motivate and encourage other human beings. He is an amazing kid!

Because of our better start, he was able to run the whole way this time, no walking *at all*. We were both very happy and proud of this achievement!

When we got close to the finish, both of us remembered how he outsprinted me last year, and I was ready for him this year. He started his sprint early, so I thought I had him, but as I pulled up on him, he switched into another gear I didn't think he had and beat me by a foot (if you can see in the picture, this is during the sprint, and he is looking back to see where I am before he makes his second effort).

Great race, overall time was a bit slower than the year before, but mostly because we went so slow in the first mile (his miles were twelve minutes, eleven, eleven, and then nine—just the way I like to race).

He ended up in third place among the ten-year-olds and was very happy, tired, sore, and hungry at the end—everything we love about running races!

Included in the race entry were tickets to the Braves' game that night. We brought his sister, Hana, and had a fantastic time and then an absolutely wonderful Father's Day the next day. I am truly blessed to be able to do this with my son. Next up is Hana for her first race!

# Pretraining for One Hundred Miles

*For the moment all discipline seems painful rather*
*than pleasant, but later it yields the peaceful fruit of*
*righteousness to those who have been trained by it.*
*Therefore lift your drooping hands and strengthen your*
*weak knees, and make straight paths for your feet,*
*so that what is lame may not be put out of joint but*
*rather be healed.*

—Hebrews 12:11–13 (esv)

## *Pretraining Program*

In late 2011 to early 2012, my training was pretty minimal in the winter and spring, mostly four- to eight-mile runs; they felt good but were nothing really long or epic.

However, I decided that things were lining up much better in 2012 to attempt one hundred miles off-road, so I looked at the Pinhoti 100 again!

God was with me on my journey again, as I was able to transfer my race entry (after some serious begging, offering to help with trail work, and a very understanding RD) for the Pinhoti 100 on November 4–5 of 2012.

It really puts running one hundred miles into perspective when the race date listed on the website covers two days!

Once I entered this race (again), I decided not to make the same mistake I did last year of doing a big race in March and then continuing with long training through the summer. By July, when the real training was to begin,

I was burnt out and could not imagine training for a hundred miler!

I absolutely *love* trail running, but it is incredible to me the people that I run with in that race do multiple fifty and hundred milers all year round!

So I enjoyed a relatively easy winter and spring by staying active, working a lot on strength training and enjoying not really having any type of plan or pressure to do long runs when I didn't feel like it.

Gotta admit, it was kinda nice, but not very inspirational or spiritual! My mind and body probably needed a long break, and so this was good, but now I was ready to start ramping it up!

## *What Does Training for a Hundred Miler Look Like?*

This is an interesting question that probably has as many different answers as the question, "What are your thoughts about solutions to the current economic situation in the US?"

Since this is such a fringe sport and has only been around for about forty years (in 2011, approximately 4,400 people completed a hundred-mile off-road running event; that's about .0001 percent of the US population, if I am doing my calculations correctly), there really are no strong data or proven training plans to go by. It's mostly blogs, personal anecdotes, etc. In fact, recently, one of the top elite ultra runners in the world was asked this question, and he—and many of the other top guys in the sport agree— basically answered, "Just do what feels right for you!"

Obviously, you have to run a lot of total miles and put in some very long training runs if you want to be competitive, but for the other 99 percent of us who just want to finish without going blind, losing a limb, or dying, the range of training plans is immense!

For instance, I have seen some people finish well on "only" thirty-five miles of running a week—crazy! On the other end of the spectrum, there are top guys who are averaging over two hundred miles per week; some of us don't even drive that much!

For me, I decided to use the six months to test my training intuition and connection to my body.

I had an off-road half marathon in mid-May that kicked off my training, but I really did not have a strict plan this time.

At one point, I tried to put it all down on an Excel spreadsheet (as I have done for previous races), and it looked so freaking daunting (using similar training volumes that worked for my fifty-three miler) that I was ready to quit running and take up shuffleboard!

I also planned on running this race for some type of charity. For me, something like this needs to be much bigger than just my personal goals, so stay tuned for more information on that.

At this early stage, I also started looking for a few good men (and women) to be pacers (after mile 40, you are allowed to have someone run with you to pace you, keep you safe, keep you awake, tell you the same jokes over and over, etc.).

It was a very important time in my life to consistently remind myself that we are *all* capable of much, much more than we think we are!

# THE NEXT JOURNEY BEGINS

*Therefore, since we are surrounded by so great a cloud
of witnesses, let us also lay aside every weight, and sin
which clings so closely, and let us run with endurance
the race that is set before us.*

—Hebrews 12:1 (ESV)

## *Commitment*

I cannot say that I began this chapter without a bit of trepidation. Excitement, fear, anticipation, etc., were all emotions swirling around my head this day. I wrote this during the week I officially (I say *officially* because really I have been training for this since I was fifteen years old) began my training program for my first attempt at a hundred-mile off-road "run."

The *run* is in quotes because the cut-off time for this race is thirty hours, which equates to an eighteen-minute-per-mile average (with stops), so it is really a jog and very fast hike (for me, anyway; some superhumans run the whole way).

Thinking of it as a fast hike was much easier to wrap my head around. If I was attempting a flat road run for one hundred miles, I would have been much, much less excited and much more fearful of dropping out.

Anyway, as I mentioned in my last book, I had been flirting with the idea of attempting a hundred-mile run for about two years before I decided to actually do it.

Well, as of this writing, that race (the Pinhoti 100) was exactly fifteen weeks away—only 105 days or 2,520 hours or 151,200 minutes or 9,072,000 seconds away, but who's counting?

I had planned (again, my plan, obviously not God's) to begin serious training about twenty weeks out, but actually this week was the first time I felt like I was training for this race.

The first week, I ran eight times (yes, you read that right). I ran six out of seven days and did two runs on two days, morning and night, for a total of 480 minutes of running what was probably about forty to fifty miles.

I don't wear a GPS or an iPod or anything that measures my distance, but I know that on most trails, I average between ten- to fourteen-minute per mile with fast walking on the steep hills, food breaks, bathroom breaks, etc., so I just divide my time by twelve to get an approximate mileage for the run. If it is a flat trail and I don't take any breaks, I divide the number by 10.

Sometimes, I get crazy and divide by 11.

But not often.

Anyway, the first week of true training was really a breakthrough for me, both physically and spiritually.

The weekend before, I went down to South Florida to visit my family and, besides making me really appreciate the trails we enjoy in Georgia after running on the flat, hot road with no sidewalk, I attended a very nice Mass on Sunday.

The message from the priest was to leave your worries at the door when you come home (he used a parable of a man who left his daily worries on his worry tree outside his home and picked them up—there were invariably many less the next day—the next morning to take them back to work). It was very well done.

I had been struggling with some stressful issues, and this helped me immensely to make my decision. If my stress affects my family adversely, I will do whatever I can to reduce that stress, and if I cannot reduce it, I will work on leaving it at the door, on my own worry tree, so it does not affect my family.

When I returned from Florida, I began my training in earnest, and this included a few days a week where I will run in the morning and at night.

Two things happened the week when I started doing this. One, for some reason, I handled the heat of the late afternoon much better (I was really dreading after-work runs). More importantly, I come home much calmer when I ran after work. Calm enough that I made a commitment that on the days (during the week) that I only run once, I would do it in the afternoon before I return to my family!

Still love my morning exercise and will continue, but this was a new thing for me.

Praise God for this powerful message!

## *A Break in the Action: The Power of Fifteen Minutes*

This may seem very strange, given the subject matter of this book (finding spiritual connections through long-distance trail running), however, I am going to write about how powerful *only 15 minutes* of exercise can be (if done correctly).

First, a quick warning. This type of training (it goes by many names—interval training, speed work, HITT, track work, etc.) is *not* for beginners. Also, make sure you are properly warmed up before you do this (the actual workout time is probably closer to twenty-five minutes if you are doing it by itself, but only fifteen if you are doing it right after a weight training workout or boot camp class, which is the *best* time do this, BTW!). Also, this is best done when well-hydrated on an empty stomach.

Anyway, there is enough detail to keep you busy for weeks in books, blogs, etc. on different types of interval workouts, so instead of giving you twenty different workouts, I will try to motivate you just to try this using a little math. If you did fifteen minutes of high-intensity intervals three times per week after your weight training workouts, you would burn, conservatively, 150 more calories per workout, plus 50 or so (depending on what study you read) more during the day after the workout. This adds up to 600 calories a week for just forty-five minutes of extra time. Keep this up for a year, and (keeping your diet consistent) this could add up to nine pounds of stubborn body fat *gone* from your body!

Do I have your attention yet?

Here is a very simple workout I have done with FormWell members (BTW, if I had a dollar for every time a member said, "I don't have time to stay after my workout to do more cardio," and then stayed around for twenty minutes, talking to their trainer or friends, I could retire and write full-time).

Trust me, if you are motivated, you have the time!

1. If you are doing this after a workout, no need to do any extra-warm up, just do two minutes of easy walking to get yourself into the flow of the treadmill (this can be done on any piece of cardio equipment and also outside, of course).

2. *Run*, preferably at an incline, at a pace that you can barely maintain for two minutes. Finding this "uncomfortable place" may take some trial and error, but basically, the feeling I am looking for is that after sixty seconds or so, you cannot wait till the two minutes are up. You are breathing very hard and can answer questions only with a quick yes, no, or inaudible grunt!

3. Walk *very slowly* for one to three minutes or until you feel totally recovered.

4. Repeat this five times.

5. Walk for two to five minutes for a cooldown and stretch.

Enjoy the afterglow. Repeat two to three times per week for maximum results.

Have fun. If you hate me during the two-minute intervals, you are doing it right!

## *It Is Not an Attempt*

At this point, it had been a month of serious training, and I was still alive!

One thing to note, I was no longer calling this race an attempt.

I was very kindly(?) reminded by one of the guys— thanks, Rob S.—in my Tuesday 5:30 a.m. strength training for endurance athletes class that calling it an *attempt* was setting myself up for failure.

Basically, I was making it *okay* if I drop out before the finish.

It was and is *not* okay. I was going to do everything I could to get to that finish line!

So I now started referring to it as just a hundred-mile *race*. The goal being to arrive at the finish line in one piece in under 30 hours and learn something about myself and God along the way!

The first five weeks were actually fantastic, training-wise. I ran, in miles (-ish), 40, 38, 47, 31 (recovery), and 51; in minutes, that's approximately 480, 456, 564, 372, and 612.

Remember, my miles are just an estimate, and I tend to estimate low (i.e., on most shorter runs, I probably average closer to 10 minutes per mile, but I still divide my total minutes by twelve to estimate my miles).

Time on my feet is what mattered most at this point in the training!

Amazingly (for me), those mileage weeks are normal for people training for marathons (26.2 miles). Ultramarathon people train 60–100 miles or more on a regular basis!

I was trusting that my years of base building and the strength I get from the awesome strength training classes in our fitness club would allow me to make it to the starting line *and* finish line fit and injury-free, even with significantly less weekly miles than most people do preparing for these events.

I obviously love running, but not 100 miles a week. Maybe when I retire, and the kids are in college!

My body was feeling really good; I had no major injuries to report (same old aches and pains but nothing new), and I was actually feeling better running than I did walking!

For example, one day, when I started a long run with a large climb at the start, it was a struggle to walk up a hill to warm up, but once I began running, I felt better. I felt strongly this must be a good sign!

I was enjoying the process and had some fun training runs planned.

Three months out from the race, I decided to clean up my diet immensely, doing APAP for the next twelve weeks (as Paleo as possible). I did great for the first week. Then it was my son's eleventh birthday, and Heather made brownies, so…you know the rest!

Going off your plan is not an end, just a simple bump in the road. Roll over that bump and move on!

Most importantly, I was working this crazy hobby, taking care of and spending quality time with my family (most Saturdays, I am done with my three- to five-hour run before they even got out of bed), working on my relationship with Jesus Christ, and trying to be focused and productive at work.

So far, God was honoring this commitment, and things were going very well!

I was also nailing down my pacers, who will stay with me after it gets dark. These men would be very important in keeping me well-fed and awake on the trail!

Other good news that occurred that week was that I finally (self) published my first book, *Quiet the Noise: A Trail Runner's Path to Hearing God*.

August 18, 2012 will always hold a special place in my heart, as that is when my mission to get this message out the world began.

I was also finalizing the e-mail blast to go out to raise money for the night shelter in Atlanta (a homeless shelter for men supported by our church).

I had decided to dedicate this run to the glory of God and use it to raise awareness and, God willing, some money to help these unfortunate homeless men.

Instead of a traditional one-time donation, I decided to have people sponsor me for a certain amount per mile.

I figured this would motivate me in the really down parts of the race that I knew would occur. Every mile I made it further would be that much more money for the homeless men.

Also, I really think that most people that pledged (a lot of nonrunning friends) were pretty confident that I would not make the entire hundred miles, so a pledge of, say, $2 per mile wouldn't cost them too much.

They obviously didn't know me very well.

# PART 2
# THE FINAL TEN WEEKS

*We can rejoice, too, when we run into problems
and trials, for we know that they help us develop
endurance.*

—Romans 5:3 (NLT)

# THE BEGINNING OF THE FINAL PUSH:
## LESSONS LEARNED

*Whatever you do, work heartily, as for the Lord and
not for men, knowing that from the Lord you will
receive the inheritance as your reward. You are serving
the Lord Christ.*

—Colossians 3:23–24 (ESV)

At this point, I was ten weeks out from my hundred-mile race. On this particular weekend, I did some great training and, at the same time, had my first real feelings of fear about this thing.

I decided it was time to practice some night running, especially on very tired legs and a tired mind. Friday, I got up for work at my normal time (4:15 a.m.), got to work at 4:45 a.m., and worked a short day till 3:00 p.m. I went home and packed up (mostly food, really funny—about ten thousand calories—and only one pair of running shorts; I have my priorities in order!)

Met a friend—Tim M., a first-time night runner—at my house (more on this later) and then another friend on the way up (Troy B., my pacer from mile 68 to the finish in Pinhoti), and we drove to a mountain bike trail at Brush Creek, just over the Tennessee border. We met another friend, Rob S. (who was to be another pacer for Pinhoti), at the trailhead at 8:00 p.m., right at dusk.

We start the run with me leading (great move, I have never been to this trail before) so I can set the pace (I was trying to slow Rob down; he is way faster than us), and I hear Tim trip in the first half mile. Then we separate from him and Troy, and he catches up and falls. Then he trips again and then takes a really nice fall right in front of me! Two trips and two nice falls in the first thirty minutes.

Tim M. is really happy he now has me as a new friend!

Turns out he was doing two things wrong (we probably should have corrected these before we started, but what fun would that be?); he had a very heavy pack with small water bottles in it; that threw his balance off.

Why he did this, I have no idea.

More importantly, he had his headlamp adjusted to far in front of him; he couldn't see right in front of his feet, so every root…well, you know!

The rest of the run was awesome. It was a new experience—running at night on a trail that was 100 percent runable, no major climbs at all.

At one point, we hit the top of the highest point, and the stars were absolutely amazing! I had not run without walking breaks in a while, except on the road, so it took some getting used to, but after about forty-five minutes, I felt fantastic.

We were planning on fourteen miles (about tree hours), but Troy was having a bad night, so we cut it off at about ten.

We saw a bunch of snakes and heard something really big in the brush next to us; Rob told us it was a wild boar. It was probably a rabid squirrel, but at night, everything is scary. We chilled out after the run with adult beverages and snacks back at the cars.

We then headed to Rob's cabin in Blue Ridge and had a nice night grilling and chilling.

Rob is an awesome cook and really likes to try out new recipes on people. We were more than willing to oblige.

Stayed up till about 1:00 a.m. (almost twenty-four hours, still working on training the sleep-deprivation thing).

Up at 6:30 a.m. Rob made us a great breakfast, and we all hit the road to different places at about 8:00 a.m.

Tim had to get home,

Rob was heading out for a brick workout made up of a three-hour mountain bike ride and a thirty-minute run.

I was heading to Fort Mountain—now made famous by my last book, *The Mystery Mountain Marathon*. If you read it, you might remember this race has about 15K of elevation change in 26.2—really 28ish—miles!

This was the same training/camping weekend I did last year. The plan is to run 12 miles on Saturday and 16 on Sunday to cover the whole course over two days.

I was planning on going home Saturday afternoon 'cause my son was having a sleepover birthday party that I didn't want to miss, so I planned on doing what any sensible ultra runner training for a hundred miler would do.

I decided to do the twelve-mile loop twice!

Luckily, the race director had planned on doing the same thing, and two others joined us.

Got to the park really early. It was really nice to not be rushed and be able to prep at my own pace.

We started our run at about 10:00 a.m. The second run was scheduled to start at 2:00 p.m. This race director is especially cruel, starting a run at 2:00 p.m. in August in Georgia!

The loop was very nice, conversational, and easy. We were in no rush to get back 'cause it would have made for more standing-around time, waiting for the other runners, which is never a good plan.

We got back around 1:20 p.m. and did our thing until the other runners (about twenty-five of them) showed up.

Here's the lesson learned here: more than a five-minute break really does not work well for me. It felt great to fuel up, pour water over my head, change shoes, etc., but I should have just started running right away and met the new group at 2:00 p.m. As it was, I started walking at about 1:45 p.m. (twenty-five-minute break) and walked about a mile till everyone started.

I wanted to see how my fitness was progressing, so I went out with the second group; the first group was way, way out of my league.

Turns out so was the second group.

And probably the third group, fourth group, AD infinitum.

Felt really, really good for about ninety minutes. Then the wheels fell off.

The heat was really getting to me, and all I could think about was getting back to the car and jumping in the cool lake!

It really was not that hot or humid for this time of year, but remember, if you read the last book, I got dehydrated and almost went blind at the Pine Mountain forty miler, and it was about thirty degrees out!

I started planning on cutting the second loop down a bit. I caught up with another runner I know, and he was feeling the same. We got to a road crossing and realized it was about one mile, all downhill, back to the cars (instead of four miles left of trails). Praise God!

Felt great running downhill on the road and felt very blessed when we finished.

Another lesson—don't wear bright colors while running on trails in Georgia in August.

A group of runners ahead of us ran through a swarm of yellow jackets, and the guy with a bright orange shirt on got stung over thirty times. He had them everywhere, even down his shorts. Ouch!

Luckily, he was not allergic, but his day was definitely over. Praise God again that there was a park ranger close who had a bee sting kit!

The people with him said when he took his shirt off and threw it away, a swarm of yellow jackets followed it!

After I got back to my car, I went straight to the lake and jumped in; it felt fantastic! I cleaned up, fueled up a bit, and hit the road. About thirty-two miles done (ten on Friday night and about twenty-two on Saturday) in less than twenty-four hours—not bad.

Anyway, two things happened this weekend.

One, I realized, as this training starts to cross over into ridiculous as far as time commitment, that this journey (until I retire) will probably be a bucket list one and done, like my Ironman experience. I was fully committed to doing the best I could on November 3–4, but after that, as I have said before, I get all the peacefulness, spiritual lessons, and quieting of my mind from shorter distances!

Also, a big spiritual lesson of the weekend was this: I need to work on prayer and connections with the Lord when I am running with others more.

I realized at about mile 20 on Saturday that I had not done a rosary or really prayed or connected to God at all the whole weekend.

There's nothing wrong with spending time with friends—fellowship is a big part of my religious journey—

but I think I can get better at staying close to God while being around others. It is just going to take training and practice like everything else.

I did manage to do one decade of the rosary on the one-mile downhill stretch at the end Saturday and then listened to the rosary app on my iPhone on the way home, so all was not lost!

Had a great night with the family on Saturday night, got in five easy miles on the road on Sunday, and enjoyed a great day at the pool and Mass on Sunday night. I was only gone twenty-four hours, and I was running for about eight of those twenty-four!

The journey continues.

## *Nine Weeks to Go: Heat and Sleep-Deprivation Training*

It never ceases to amaze me that after over thirty-five years of running, I can still have *another* new experience!

As I mentioned earlier, one of the suggestions from the five hundred different training plans for one hundred milers on the Internet included practicing sleep deprivation. The thought of staying up for thirty-plus hours, running for most of it, is one of the scariest things for me about this run.

So I figured practice might help!

FYI, I don't believe you can really train your body to perform well when it is exhausted; however, you can train your mind, your spirit, and your will to overcome the exhaustion and persevere!

So here is an outline of a week/weekend training.

Monday to Wednesday were normal days,

Monday was a complete day off.

Tuesday, I did a six-mile run.

Wednesday, I had a 5:00 a.m. strength training workout and very short run in afternoon.

The weekend really started on Thursday. That day, I ran six miles in the morning (hilly and slow) and five miles at night (flat and fast).

Went to bed about 11:00 p.m. and got up at 4:15 a.m. for work Friday. Trained with a client at 5:30 a.m. (lightweight training workout) and worked a nice short day, ending about 3:00 p.m.

Like the week before, I stayed on my feet from 3:00 p.m. till 6:00 p.m., and then headed out to a new trail to meet a friend to do a night run.

I was very, very tired (falling-asleep-at-the-wheel kind of tired) when driving there, but immediately, when I started running, I felt better.

Blankets Creek was a new running trail for me (I have mountain biked here before), and I started my run during the day, when there were a lot of mountain bikers there.

Very, very interesting and a bit unnerving.

The trail is so narrow that when you run or hike, you have to go the opposite way of the mountain bikers and basically stop and get off the trail when they come by (they have the right of way).

It's pretty easy when they are going uphill, but when they are blasting the downhills, it got a little close a few times. I had my music on and decided to drop one of my earbuds, so I could hear them coming. That helped a bit.

Did about 5.5 miles in a little over an hour; lots of stopping slowed me down. I then met Troy B., my main pacer for Pinhoti, to do another lap.

Fueled up with some carbs and caffeine; I felt great and started second loop.

I need to mention here that this night might have been the most humid it had been all summer. When we turned on our headlamps, it was like you were running through a swarm of bugs; there was so much moisture in the air!

Troy and I both sweat a lot.

Okay, no one on earth sweats more than Troy, but I am close, so carrying water was a very good idea, even for only 5.5 miles.

The second loop was actually much easier than the first. The trail was almost completely cleared of mountain bikers, and the ones who were still there had headlamps also, so you could see them coming a mile away.

We did run into two guys riding without lights. That was interesting. I still wonder if they made it back to the parking lot alive!

Finished 11 miles, loaded up on protein and carbs, and headed home.

Took a shower, had one beer (I was not hungry at all—not a good thing 'cause I had another run planned for Saturday morning), and went to bed.

Unfortunately, the caffeinated gels and Mountain Dew I drank during the run kicked in, and I didn't fall asleep till after midnight.

The plan was to get up at 5:00 a.m. and start running again by 6:00 a.m. I overslept a bit till 5:30 a.m. and hit the trail by 6:45 a.m.

So, over two days, I got about ten hours sleep.

Not a big deal for some people, but I am a person who needs eight-plus hours a night to function well, so I was *definitely* sleep deprived!

Saturday morning was even more humid than Friday night (side note: I learned what the dew point actually means; it was seventy-one degrees out, and the dew point was seventy, so, basically, 99 percent humidity).

The plan was five hours at Kennesaw Mountain, but I was done after three! The heat was really getting to me, and I didn't want to push too hard and get sick or injured!

Went home and passed out for two hours and then had an awesome weekend with the family—an easy five-mile road run Sunday morning and great day biking with Heather, the kids, and friends on the Silver Comet trail Monday (very slow and easy).

It was a good confidence-building weekend in terms of back-to-back long runs and sleep deprivation.

However, I felt very far behind, not in total miles but in my long runs. I had a fifty-mile race (this would be my longest training run) coming up in three weeks, and I had not run more than four hours in almost a year. This race would take me at least twelve hours, so I would see how my physical, spiritual, and mental training was really going!

Because I was running with others most of the time—and when I was solo, I was dodging flying mountain bikers—I didn't have any big religious moments during this training week.

However, I was able to pray more, even with others around, and that is a good improvement from the week before!

At this point in my journey, I was really pushing hard to get some of my Catholic brothers out there with me. It would be great to be able do discuss the Lord, Bible, etc. while running. I continue to pray that this starts to happen soon.

Perhaps if I cut my runs down to three to six miles instead of twenty to twenty-five more people will be willing/able to join me!

On a final note, since I was starting to get nervous and there are only a little over eight weeks to go as of this writing, I reached out to my coach, Matt R., for some guidance as we get closer. He tweaked my planned training just a bit, and it gave me some confidence that I might not be as far off as I thought!

## *Eight Weeks to Go: The Weather*

What a difference one day, a drop in temperature, and humidity can make.

At this stage in my training for my hundred miler, my plan called for a recovery week. This equated to less days running (only ran four out of seven days) and about a 20 percent drop in the average total miles in my last three weeks (I averaged fifty-two miles a week so that means I was to do about forty-two miles this week).

I still planned on doing back-to-back long runs, as this is where I felt very behind in my training.

I did two very easy six-mile runs during the week, which left me about thirty miles do to over the weekend—perfect!

On Saturday, I ran down at the river, about sixty minutes with a buddy and then about two more hours solo. It was really tough. I did all flat roads and trails. I have not run like that in a while, and it was very hot and humid. I felt good for about ninety minutes and then the wheels fell off. Couldn't wait to be done and cut my run short at about 14 miles and two hours forty-five minutes.

Fueled up and let the down feeling go. It was gonna be a great day Sunday.

Sunday morning, I was running with a group at one of my favorite trails in Georgia—the approach trail to the start of the Appalachian Trail (Amicalola Falls to top of Springer Mountain, over to Hike Inn for snacks, and back) It's 17ish miles, with 2,300 feet of elevation gain in the first 7.5 miles; it's affectionately called the Meat Grinder!

The weather completely changed overnight, and it was only fifty-five degrees and low humidity when I got up at 5:00 a.m. to get ready.

Tried something new for breakfast—salami, cheese and mayo on white bread, and a banana. It was *awesome* and kept me full for a very, very long time! May be my new pre–long run meal!

A new buddy, Tim M., famous for falling four times in 1 mile on his first night run with us, was supposed to meet me at my house at 5:30 a.m.; it was about an hour's drive up, and the start time was 7:00 a.m. At 5:31 a.m., I texted him, and he says he was on his way. I found out later he had been out drinking till 3:00 a.m. and was still sleeping when I texted him—nice training plan!

Anyway, we make it up there and begin the run with about fifteen other people at 7:00 a.m. It is actually cold up there. I could have worn a long-sleeved shirt! This is my favorite weather to run in, and I felt great right from the start. I really could have run all day on this day! The hills felt so much easier than the last time I was up there, and the descents were fun, as always. We made it to the top of Springer in under two hours, had a quick snack, and headed back.

Now did I mention to you that Tim M. had been drinking till 3:00 a.m. the night before? This guy is amazing in his ability to party and then get up and run. He reminds me a lot of me in college.

Except for the getting-up-the-next-morning-and-running part!

He was actually doing very, very well for about the first 10 miles (he ate no breakfast also) and then he started to drop back a bit on all the climbs. Being a very good and caring wingman, I waited for him at the top of each climb to make sure he was okay. I also got him food and electrolyte pills when he needed them. With about a mile to go, he decides to thank me for all my attentiveness and caring efforts.

He takes off.

He proceeds to run up a hill that I was walking up. I figure he will wait at the top, like I did. Nope.

He continues to take off.

I almost caught him at the end, but bottom line, I learned some valuable lessons this day.

1. Never wait for Tim again at the top of hills.

2. Never give Tim and water, food, or electrolyte pills.

3. Go out till 3:00 a.m. before my next run and let wine be my carbohydrate; it obviously works.

4. Don't run too close to people who drank a lot the night before; they stink.

5. Never wait for Tim again.

To top things off, when we get back, Tim's car has a flat tire. He has no idea how to change it, so I do all the work, including asking a park ranger for help getting the spare off the car!

*And* reading instructions!

Very humiliating!

On a serious note, this was the best I have felt yet in my training for Pinhoti, and it was a nice confidence builder. Also, while Tim was dying (did I mention he was toast after ten miles and only found his way back to the car 'cause I *waited* for him at the top of every climb?), we stopped talking altogether, and I was able to do a full rosary while running with someone else, which was very, very cool.

I felt God all along this run and remembered, in a very clear way, why I do this stuff. Sometimes, I think I should just run from September to April and take up golf for the summer months!

Yeah, right.

## *Seven Weeks to Go: Alone*

It's Friday night, September 14, 2012. I can still remember when Friday nights meant early happy hour and late nights out dancing and having fun in bars and parties.

Well, I now have a different type of happy hour!

On this day, I got out of work early and headed up to the mountains for a weekend of camping, running, camping, having fun with family, more running, and some hiking.

I arrived at Amicalola Falls State Park at around 4:00 p.m. on Friday. I was thinking about doing a night run, but the thought of being out there all alone, without any protection (except my severely atrophied arms), against the bears and other wildlife, made me decide to get it done early. I do a lot of my running alone, but it is normally in parks where I see a lot of other people.

Not this day/evening!

Started my run at about 5:00 p.m. The plan was to run one hour out or get to Hike Inn (about a five-mile run), whichever came first, and turn around. This was a new trail for me (starts the same as last week's approach trail to the start of the AT), and I was excited about the new terrain and sights!

The trail was very nice and nontechnical (by North Georgia Mountain standards), and I felt great right from the start (unique for me 'cause it normally takes me about an hour to warm up and feel good).

Mentally/spiritually, I had some anxiety and distracted thinking on the drive up, so I had decided to do my daily "running" rosary in the car before I got to my campsite. This really is a gift from God (and my friend, Chris M., who introduced me to it)! It calmed me right down and put me in a good frame of mind for the weekend.

Anyway, back to the run. I was a bit paranoid running by myself, and I had not purchased a bear bell, which was suggested by friends who run up here all the time. Basically, you don't want to ever surprise a bear, and the bell warns them that you are coming so they can get off the trail and decide not to eat you.

I was constantly looking and praying I wouldn't come around a corner and surprise a big momma bear or daddy bear! I decided to play music in my iPhone so the bears could hear me coming, hoping they dislike Christian rock and would run away from the sound!

This worked well to alleviate some of my nervousness. However, the music was on satellite radio that would come and go unexpectedly. It would shut off for a while and then come on, loud, with no warning. I almost jumped off the trail a couple of times.

Definitely kept me awake and alert.

I was very surprised to see one hour on my watch. Time flew out there, and I was not quite at Hike Inn yet. I really thought I would reach it in under an hour; however, it turns out the first two miles of this trail are almost all uphill, which slowed me considerably. So I got to mile marker 4.3 and turned around.

The run back was *fantastic*! My legs felt strong and injury-free. Hydration and nutrition was spot-on, and I made it back in just under fifty-five minutes! So here is the coolest thing about this run: I ran two hours and did not see one other human being!

Not one.

At one point, I stopped where there was a break in the trees to snap a picture of a beautiful view, and it was so cool to hear *nothing* except the sounds of nature. You could hear all the crickets and animals and the wind whistling through the trees.

At one point after this, I had a mental conversation/ prayer session with my dad (gone twenty years this past May 3), and I feel like he really spoke to me. He told me he was at peace and proud of me. Brought me to tears, for sure. This was really an amazing, unexpected run.

I got back at about 7:00 p.m. and had about an hour of daylight to set up camp and make dinner (I also wrote this chapter in pen—man, that hurt; hand's not used to writing). I took a hot shower (obviously, this was not primitive camping) and chilled by the fire with a nice cold adult beverage.

One of the amazing things about running alone and then camping alone is how much time slows down. You have no agenda and no one asking you to do things or be somewhere.

There is no rush.

There is nowhere to be at a certain time.

I actually had a moment where I just stared at a butterfly for almost a minute, just appreciating the moment and the beauty of God's nature. When does this *ever* happen in our noisy, hectic lives? As I have said many times, we all find our way to these peaceful moments; mine just happens to be during and after runs in nature.

God is good!

Saturday morning, Troy B., my pacer for the final thirty-one miles of my upcoming hundred mile suffer-fest, met me to run the Meat Grinder again (I had run it the weekend previously).

Nothing particular stood out on this day, except that I did not feel very strong for the first two hours and felt *amazing* for the last two hours.

The family was meeting me after this run to have a nice day, hiking, relaxing, etc. and then my daughter was going to camp with me Saturday night. We had a great time. It is so nice to be able to hike with Heather again (she just had a hip replacement and is doing great), and the kids did great. At one point, they both took off downhill and beat us back to the start by over five minutes—trail runners in training!

Had a wonderful nonrushed and peaceful weekend—some great alone time, time with a friend, family time, and then alone time with my daughter.

I am truly blessed.

# *Six Weeks to Go: Confidence Builder and Confidence Shaker*

The week of September 17, 2012, was very interesting in terms of training and my first real test of fitness and readiness. The goal was to run about twenty easy miles during the week (I was pretty trashed from last week) and then compete in a fifty-mile race (The Georgia Jewel) on Saturday. This race is run on the Georgia section of the Pinhoti Trail and has very similar elevation change and terrain to what I would be running in November.

Although only half the distance!

The week went well. It was really strange (perception is reality, I suppose) that I was not really nervous or thinking about this race much. In March 2011, in what had been my longest ever run then, I was *very* nervous.

Last year, I tapered for three weeks, totally prepared the week of the race with nutrition, sleep, etc.

This year, I trained right up till race day, didn't get a whole lot of sleep, and didn't eat as well as I could have.

In fact, I didn't even know where the race was being held till about a week before (Dalton, Georgia, FYI)! Obviously, with my upcoming hundred miler, this race was a "training day" to see how I was doing.

Friday night, I prepped my drop bag (a bag you give to the race director to drive out to a aid station with your favorite food, change of socks, pain killers, etc.) and got into bed at 6:30 p.m. Yes, 7:00 p.m. was my projected time to be asleep, as my alarm was set for 2:45 a.m. Saturday morning!

This race was ninety minutes away, and I had to be there at 5:00 a.m.! Actually fell asleep with no problem and got up feeling awesome.

Got ready and was at the race site a bit early. Funny, *now* I started to get nervous. Not so much about the race or distance, more about making sure I had everything I needed.

Ironically, that is the one thing I really didn't need to get nervous about; anything I might have forgotten, they had out on the course.

If I had been smart and actually reviewed the elevation change and terrain of this course – *that* is what should have made me nervous!

We started in the dark at 6:00 a.m. There was also a 35-mile race going on. They started with us and a hundred miler. They started at 4:00 a.m. Imagine when they had to get up!

The course started out very uniquely (for me, anyway) with a 1.3-mile climb on a road before we hit the trails. It was very cool to look back and see all these headlamps running up the street; it must have been quite a sight for cars driving the other way. The trail then went off road, right on to a jeep trail, and to another mile or so of climbing (I think, may have been shorter, but distances are weird when it is dark).

We all kept saying, "These two miles (or so) downhill is going to be really fun at mile 48, when we have no quads left to help us run downhill!"

Anyway, we then finally hit the single track, and OMG, this was a technical trail. I have run on rockier, but never for this long (and in the dark). It felt like at least 10 miles of sharp, jagged, and nasty rocks up and down hills. Did I mention in the dark?

Did I mention rocks?

The most common Facebook post I have seen on this race was about having nightmares about rocks.

I ran with some people for a while, but I realized that going at someone else's pace (whether slower or faster than my normal pace) was really messing up my gait, and after almost falling three times, I passed the group I was with and headed out on my own.

Of course, right after it got light out, I took a very nice fall—all by myself.

God was with me, as it was not a very rocky section, but I managed to fall in between some rocks and a tree. I was a little banged up but nothing too bad. More dirt on my body than anything!

I also smashed my toe so bad one time that I saw stars and almost took a tumble face-first into a tree.

Other than that, the first twenty-five miles were pretty uneventful.

I was really feeling good and pushing the pace (again, for me, pushing the pace is probably a 12-minute mile on these trails) for the first half of the race. I decided early on to not eat or drink as much as normal and push myself harder than normal to see what my 100-mile training body is now capable of. I figured if I fell apart, there would always be someone out there that could take me back to my car!

I don't have a GPS, but I knew we were getting close to the 25-mile turnaround based on the aid stations and how long I had been running, and something *very* strange was happening.

I was not seeing the leaders of the race coming back (this was an out-and-back course).

I did some math and figured they should be about four to five miles ahead of me at the turnaround. I actually didn't see the leader until about one mile from the turnaround point! So now my mind starts playing tricks on me.

I must have taken a wrong turn.

Maybe they didn't come back the exact same way as we went out (I know, that makes no sense, but this is what happens to your brain after five hours of running).

So I ended up seeing about eight to ten people, including the top two females, coming down the climb (it was a very cool, long climb up to the twenty-five-mile point), and I finally admitted to myself that I was in the top 10, overall, in the race!

Now this is not such a big deal for some people, but it was a shocker to me! Of course, I just chalked it up to going out so hard for the first half and figured thirty people would pass me on the way back (not sure how many were in my race, but it wasn't that many, obviously).

Either that or there were only ten people in the fifty miler!

I got to the turnaround in five hours and twenty-seven minutes (at a pace that was over an hour faster than my last fifty miler on a much tougher course, except for the mud, of course).

Fueled up, enjoyed a beautiful view from the top of the mountain, and headed back down.

I really loved the top of this mountain, especially coming down. It was very sparse, sunny, and it felt like I was were in Colorado or Washington State—pine trees and everything! If it weren't for the *huge* rocky steps we had to go down, it was a perfect trail running moment.

Saw a bunch of people I know on the way down, and there were lots of words of encouragement that helped me a ton and kept me running when I thought about walking.

Up to this point, I was doing very well physically and mentally.

Except for my feet.

The bottoms of my feet started to really hurt after only ten miles on this gnarly trail. On my left foot, I knew, was a huge blister that I always get after about three hours of running. But my right foot was a different story; there was a burning sensation just behind the big toe that was very, very painful.

On a good note, it got so bad that I completely forgot about my chronic Achilles pain in my right foot!

I passed a few people on the way back (not that I was running faster; I'd slowed considerably, but they must have slowed more than me) and was still feeling good, but the pain in my right foot just kept escalating. At a few points, I had to stop, hold on to a tree, and lift my foot up to take the pressure off because it hurt so badly.

After about thirty miles, I was pretty sure I could finish, and I was still running okay. Only one person had passed me (female), so I figured everyone else in the race got lost, quit, or were having as much trouble with their feet as I was.

I knew I was getting close to the finish and passed a guy that was in the thirty-five-mile race. He told me he trained on the course all the time, and we had just one more climb till the downhill all the way to the finish. I picked it up and tried to run all the downhills and flat sections, even a few of the gentle uphills.

I got to the top of the last climb and met up with a woman who I had seen all throughout the race. She was having terrible stomach problems. I helped her get some salt pills, offered some water (she could not swallow either), and then realized what she really needed was to be left alone so she could collect herself, maybe puke, and then make it to the finish!

Now it was downhill all the way to the finish.

There are two things I want to stress here.

First, my feet were *beyond* painful now, and downhill running was the worst, but at least it was not technical, and there were no more rocks.

Second, I had this feeling that everyone I passed was right behind me, so I was sprinting down the hill and looking behind me the whole time. I think it was actually over ten minutes before the next man came over the finish line, so I was safe, but you never know!

I could not wait to get to the finish line and take off my shoes. I crossed the line and, much to my absolute amazement and disbelief, get handed the trophy for third overall male!

Crazy, I was thinking I might win my age group, as I knew there were only a few people ahead of me, but I never, ever expected top 3 *overall*! Not sure of my time 'cause I didn't stop my watch and there was no race clock (that I saw), but I think it was somewhere around eleven hours, forty minutes.

Sat down, (OMG, that felt good), took off my shoes, and drank three—yes, three—real sodas; I had one Coke, one Orange, and one Sprite! Also had a McDonalds hamburger; it really hit the spot.

All I was craving was something bubbly and cold. I had been drinking lukewarm water with salt/potassium pills for almost twelve hours.

BTW, this was a hot race for me also (about sixty at the start and warmed up to over eighty), and I did not have any real hydration or overheating problems! Training through the summer must have helped. Trust me, I would much rather run in the cool weather, but this gave me some confidence if we happened to have a freak warm day in November.

Here are the lessons from the race:

Mentally, I came to some conclusions and gave myself some freedoms in this race. The pain in my feet was so bad that I know that if this had been one hundred miles, I would *not* have been able to finish. I can handle a decent amount of pain, but when it feels like burning needles in your feet every time you hit the ground, I'm pretty sure I had found my pain-tolerance limit!

So, at about mile 40, I made a deal with myself. I would do everything in my power to finish today. If I had a day like this in Pinhoti, even though I feel a strong sense of obligation to finish to raise the most money possible for the homeless men, I would *not* risk permanent injury to finish the hundred miles. Mentally, this helped me a lot.

I have never, ever DNFed a race, but if my first does occur in my hundred-mile race, I will do my best to accept it as God's will and move on.

That being said, I resolved to spend the next six weeks experimenting with different shoe and sock variations. I resolved to focus more on my diet to drop some weight, which cannot hurt regarding foot impact. I resolved (again) to train my butt off, adding more long efforts on rocky terrain to train my feet. Also, I planned on changing my shoes once during the race and my socks multiple times (this seemed to help a lot of people out there).

I was still going to do everything in my power to finish the race on November 3 to 4. I was just allowing myself the freedom to pull out if it gets dangerous!

From a spiritual and mental standpoint, I had a good day. The first six hours, even with the pain, were very steady. Lots of nice prayer time, two full rosaries, lots of appreciating God's beauty, and feeling blessed to be able to do what I was doing. The next six hours were an emotional roller coaster; however, three things got me right out of the low times.

1.  Nutrition

    After six hours, I really become disinterested in food, and I was eating much less than normal. When I would start to feel down mentally, I would take a break to eat a gel or some food and would feel better within five minutes (note to pacers reading this, when my mood goes down, make sure I take in some sugar, salt, and fat, if possible)!

2.  Perspective

    When the pain got really bad, I would just think (and pray for) of the homeless men in Atlanta. They have it so hard every single day. My pain was/is temporary, and I was heading home to a great house, a warm bed, and an awesome family. That put things in perspective and pushed me on.

3.  Perception of pain.

    The day before my race, I went to see a good friend of mine who is an applied kinesiologist to work on my back, which was really tight, and my Achilles, which is even tighter. We talked about pain, and he shared with me the medical definition of pain (I am sure I will butcher this)—"An *emotional* response to a nerve stimulus from real or *perceived* tissue trauma." I would repeat this mantra in my head (between rosaries and prayers), and the pain would just magically go away! Pain is an emotional response; we *can* control it (to a point)!

So now I was looking at a *huge* third place plaque and enjoying some wonderful postrace nutrition and Advil.

I was feeling confident in my race performance, elated in how I finished.

I was, at the same time, feeling *very* scared about my feet.

Overall, I was feeling very okay and centered with all these emotions. Another cool thing that came to me in this race (since it was so small, and I spent so much time running alone)—was that I *really* need and enjoy fellowship every hour or so during these things.

Mentally, I try not to think about running fifty miles. I think of running from aid station to aid station. This race had a few unmanned water stations that just didn't quite give me the uplift that I get when I see humans! As a bonus, being able to see my family and friends during the hundred miler will be a much-needed and appreciated break in the action, so to speak.

It is God's will. On November 3 and 4, I would do the best I could, but I would not put myself in the hospital in order to finish.

PS: I logged seventy-one total miles for the week—the most ever, by far, in my life. Recovery week was planned for the next week. Praise God. Even if it was not planned, it would have to happen as I could barely walk, much less hit the trails with those hamburger feet.

# Five Weeks to Go: Recovery

Not much to write about this week. I really could barely walk on Sunday after my fifty miler. On Monday, took another complete day off. Tuesday, I did an hour on the stationary bike, the first time in about six months. It felt good to spin the legs out. Wednesday, I went for my first run, five miles on the road; it felt horrible, but better at the end. Thursday morning, I did a very easy two hours on the trails and felt much better. Then I had a *huge* church weekend (a retreat called Christ Renews His Parish or CRHP), so I barely ran at all over the weekend. Ended up with twenty-three total miles, my lightest week in about four months—scary, but I really had no choice.

For next week, the plan was to get back to serious training and traveling to Napa for a much-needed vacation; I planned to get some great miles in California!

# Four Weeks to Go: Napa

A month before the race, my wife and I got to take our first real vacation without the kids in four years. Praise God!

One of our good friends and clients has a house in Napa, California, that he let us use for five days, and I was able to use frequent flyer miles to get us out there, so there we went! Monday and Tuesday, before we headed out of town, were a blur. I was trying to get five days' work done in two. I got in three runs but not much mileage.

We left Wednesday early morning. I managed to squeeze a five-mile loop run at 4:30 a.m. (ten half-mile loops around our neighborhood). It was actually not bad. I kept my mind in the game as I was counting Hail Marys at the same time I was counting laps—multitasking, for sure!

We got to California and headed right to San Francisco via a very nice ferry ride. It was nice to walk around the city that I love so much and where we spent three days of our honeymoon (we actually got to have drinks in the hotel where we stayed—nice memories). Also got another three miles of very hilly walking in; added it to the training log!

Thursday, I got up at 10:30 a.m. after the most amazing ten hours of sleep I have had in months (really 7:30 a.m. California time) and prepped for my first California trail run!

I was planning on doing the famous Dipsea trail—a seven-mile trail that actually has one of the, if not the, oldest trail races in the United States run on it each year. If you ever want to look up a unique race, check it out. They handicap the fast runners by making them start way back, thus giving everyone a chance to win the race (in fact, one year, the race battle for first was between a nine-year-old girl and a sixty-five-year-old woman; the nine-year-old won!).

Plans changed, as I didn't look ahead and realized that it was over an hour's drive each way. With a six-hour run planned, I didn't want Heather to have to wait eight-plus hours to do something together. I found a park about twenty minutes from my friend's house and had Heather drop me off. It looked like a fourteen-mile trail, so figured I would do it twice for my long one this week.

It was a very interesting trail. First of all, there is a sign when you start—"Beware of rattlesnakes, wild pigs, and mountain lions." Nice! Then it basically goes uphill, very steep (unrunnable for this guy) for about two miles, right out of the parking lot.

It had not rained here in a while, so the trail was very dry and dusty (my poor new Cascadias!), which made it slippery on the corners. This looked like more of a mountain bike trail than a running trail (there was a large group out there hiking, but I was the only crazy one running this trail). Went through some very cool areas with a real wilderness feel, but most of the trail was exposed and kind of barren—not really my thing.

At one point, you went through a gate onto private property. I was wondering why you had to keep the gate closed until I came around a corner, and *bam!* There are three cows right in the middle of the trail!

They looked at me like I was crazy. I looked at them like, "What are cows doing on the trail?" Then we both moved on.

The rest of this loop was pretty uneventful. The trail really didn't appeal to me or bring me any spiritual insights, but it was definitely cool to be in a very, very different environment. Also made me appreciate, again, the wonderful secluded trails we have in Georgia!

Got back to the parking lot after about 2.5 hours, fueled up, and headed back out. I had planned on six hours, but it started to get really warm, and I wasn't digging the trail, so I decided to take a different trail (this one said on the map, "Very steep and narrow trail") and see if I could make the run harder and shorter.

I did.

This part of the trail, the Rim-something trail, was *brutal.* It basically went straight up a mountain. At one point, I had to rest leaning and holding on to a tree 'cause if I didn't, I would have fallen back down the mountain.

The views were amazing and sometimes scary, and I had many connections to the Lord on this climb!

At the top, I actually took my hydration pack off, sat down on a rock, and had something to eat. My legs were rubber, and I was starving, and more importantly, I was not in any hurry to be anywhere.

Praise God for vacations!

Down the mountain was tough; it was not as steep as the other side, but still very tough to let the legs go and really run. Finished up on a road and ended up with 4.5 hours of running, probably about twenty to twenty-two miles. Not bad.

Again, today, I was reminded that my connection with nature occurs mostly when I am surrounded by trees in a dark forest.

Being exposed in a barren, desert-like landscape is different, but it doesn't let my mind wander and hear the Lord as much as in secluded trails.

The plan was still, later this week, to attempt to make it to Dipsea. Looking at pictures, that trail looked much more to my liking.

BTW, day 3 in Napa was an eight-mile road run. It was a beautiful road but had absolutely no shoulder, so it was pretty scary when trucks came by. Four miles basically uphill out and turn around; it took forty-five minutes out and about thirty-three back.

## *Dipsea*

Saturday, on our Napa trip, it was time to travel a bit to experience some famous California trails! I had planned on making the Dipsea trail (site of the oldest trail race in the United States) my semilong run for the week.

Woke up and decided (sort of) not to run Dipsea based on recommendations on the race website. Most of the site described how hard the trail was to follow and that you should really run it the first time with someone who has run it before.

I really didn't want to spend my morning looking for my way and feeling lost, so we decided to go to the local Napa running store and ask for a good place to experience California trails.

The people there were very nice, but only one guy really seemed like he knew what he was talking about, and he was a fellow trail runner, so I decided to listen to him! After a few suggestions of going to the Marin Trail Head, he then mentioned Dipsea as the *best* place to run.

I told him my concerns, and he said, "It is *so* easy. You really *cannot* get lost. Whenever you get to a trail crossing, it will be *obvious* where to go, or there *will* be someone there you can ask."

Can you tell where this is going?

Foreshadowing?

Famous last words?

So we drove over (said it was a one hour's drive but took 1.5 hours—another sign for sure), and it took us a while just to find the trailhead. He told me that was because land is so valuable in California that you won't find a lot of parking lots or parks associated with trails.

Boy, he was right.

Somehow, we found a trailhead (not the actual start) and parked. Thank God Heather was with me 'cause I would have gone the wrong way right from the start (she has an amazing sense of direction; I get lost in my own driveway). We walked together about fifteen minutes and then my legs were itching to go, and I took off.

(Our, not God's) plan was that she would meet me at the other end of the trail (Stinson Beach) in about two hours, allowing me to take my time and enjoy the journey!

The beginning of the trail was great. Then I came out onto a road and had no idea where to go.

Note to self: next time you do this, *bring a trail map!*

I wandered back and forth in this area. Turns out I was near the Muir Forest park. Finally, I found a trailhead that was marked Dipsea and showed I was on my way to Stinson Beach.

Okay, cool, about an extra half mile of running, and I was back on track.

Then I hit another road.

Then I could not find the trail.

I found the trailhead, but it was no longer the Dipsea trail. I seemed to remember something from the website that said you went on different trail for a while, so I decided to take a risk. This trail was really cool—mostly in the woods, very flat and runnable, and went on for about two miles before I hit *another* road!

Now I am about sixty minutes into the run and nowhere near the Dipsea trail (I think). Again, I wander around for a while and come across a guy running the other way. I ask him how to get to Stinson Beach, and he says I can go on some other trails (cannot remember name right now) that include a 4.5-mile climb over the mountains that run along the beach. Sounds awesome!

Now it gets really cool and scary at the same time. This trail was basically a switchback up a mountain, mostly exposed, and I was able to run pretty much the whole way. I am in great shape at this point in my training. The awesome weather and no humidity really helped! As I approached the top of the climb, it got even cooler (actually and metaphorically).

You could feel a change in the temperature and see mist coming off the Pacific Ocean as you neared the top (or what I thought was the top).

Got to a vista where you could see the climb I just did and the ocean on the other side. Amazing!

I would have enjoyed it a lot more if I had any idea where I was.

God was with me because as I came back from the vista, I saw a sign that said 2.5 Miles to Dipsea Trail! I would not have seen this sign if I had not gone off the trail to enjoy the great view. Before that, I was planning on following signs to Muir Beach, which looked like it was 1 mile on a busy road to get there; it was not really what I was looking for to end my run!

Anyway, I headed down the trail and…

It kept going up!

I should have realized it 'cause it definitely was not 4.5 miles of uphill running by the time I saw this sign.

I asked a couple of mountain bikers if I was on the right track to head to Stinson Beach, and they had no idea. They did say that in about 3 miles, I would hit a dirt road that would take me back to civilization and then I could go about 6 miles to Mill Valley.

Did I mention that Mill Valley was where I started?

I continued running and just tried to enjoy the trail and the moment. I won't lie. There were moments where I started to question whether this was a good idea to do alone.

Especially with my sense of direction and no trail map.

Finally, I see the crossroad and there are other people hiking there. Praise God!

I stop to check in with a couple, and they have a map (what a novel idea). They are also headed to Stinson Beach, and we realize I am only about fifty feet from the Dipsea and then it is 3 miles of mostly downhill to the beach!

Praise God again!

I am about two hours into the run now and finally have a cell signal, sent Heather a text that I am only 3 miles away.

The rest of the run was a complete joy. A mix of very fast, nontechnical downhills out in the open with beautiful, dark forest sections with redwoods, dark green moss, and huge ferns. It was absolutely amazing and what I pictured running in Northern California!

At this point, I didn't want the run to end.

I was feeling as good as I have throughout this whole training program. My legs felt strong, I was hardly sweating at all, and my Achilles felt good. It couldn't get much better!

I arrived into the town of Stinson Beach and went right to a beachside café, called Heather, and got a large ice cream cone. It was amazing!

This run ended up being 2.5 hours, about 11 miles by my estimate.

The lesson here was to let go and let God.

When I was worried about where I was, I wasn't enjoying the run or scenery as much. I kept trying to go with the flow and accept that I was lost for a reason. I was able to get in some amazing hill training, built a lot of confidence in my fitness level, and appreciate how well my body is functioning at this point in my training.

Four weeks to go—two tough, two taper.

Excited and nervous in equal doses!

## *Sixteen Days to Go: Getting Calm*

At this point in my training, I could not believe I only had a little over two weeks before my hundred-mile race!

When I started seriously attacking my training program about sixteen weeks previous to this, it seemed like I had all the time in the world! At this point, it felt like the time had passed in a blink of an eye.

Definite metaphor for life!

With four weeks to go, I had my hardest week planned, both in terms of miles and logistically (after all, as much as I might think I am a professional athlete, I am far from it and still have to be a husband, dad, and business owner)! The plan was a total of eighty miles for the week with two back-to-back runs of thirty miles or six hours each.

I had no illusions that this would actually happen, as I had a camping trip planned with my son for Saturday and Sunday, so I had to do almost all the training in five days instead of seven.

Eighty miles in five days?

Okay for normal ultra runners but a big stretch for me.

I managed to get in sixty-five total miles before the weekend, and I took Monday completely off. Yep, sixty-five miles in four days.

Again, this is a pretty regular, tame week for most of the people I would be racing with, but for me, it was a ton of volume in a short period of time.

My two long runs looked like this: Thursday morning (my late day at work), I started running at 6:00 a.m. and ran for five hours (twenty-five to thirty miles, not really sure but gave myself credit for twenty-five to be safe) down at a local park.

This was one of the few days during this training program that I did not really feel like running. Physically, I was beat; mentally, I was not into it; and spiritually, I was a bit out of it.

The beauty of this crazy goal is I really didn't have a choice, not this close to race day. For all my long-distance efforts (Ironman, Half Ironmans, marathons, ultras) the third and fourth weeks out are usually the hardest.

And the most important.

So I dragged myself out of bed, had some organic salami, cheese, and a banana for breakfast (yummy) and hit the trails. A friend was meeting me sometime during the run, so I was looking forward to some company.

The beginning of the run was really tough. It was actually a bit cold, and I was underdressed. It was dark, and it seemed like everything in my body hurt, especially my lame old feet.

I pushed on and began doing my rosary, which always settles my mind. I try to only pray for others when I pray to Mary. I think it is really good to get out of my own issues and think of those less fortunate.

As the run progressed (duh), I started to feel better and better. In fact, by the time my friend showed up (I had been running for four hours), I felt fantastic and felt like I could have run all day (good thing, 'cause that is what I will be doing soon)! I Finished up. I really could have done more without any problem, but I had to get to work.

I feel pretty confident in saying I was one of the few people in Atlanta that morning who did a five-hour run before work!

The next day, I had a night run with friends.

Again, driving to the mountain bike trails we have been doing our night runs on, I was not into it. Friday afternoon, I was exhausted from the week of work and training and really just wanted to stay on the couch and watch some really bad TV.

Again, that was not a choice at this point in the training.

Started my run at 4:00 p.m. and planned on running till at least 9:00 p.m. (again, meeting some training buddies, one of whom will be my major pacer in the race—Troy B.). Ran about two hours by myself and, again (duh), felt great after about an hour. This could be due to the training, or it could be that I was trying out some Nodoz that I will be using during the race; that really worked, I can tell you!

Ran back to the parking lot to meet my buds at about 6:00 p.m.

A funny story during the run—I had my cell phone with me (so I could let them know if I was running late), and I get a prank call. It was very funny, very well-done, and from a blocked number.

Turns out my eleven-year-old son figured out how to make the number blocked on mom's phone. It cracked me up while running against mountain bike traffic—awesome!

I picked up my two friends and started lap 3 (they were about 5.5-mile loops). Well, I thought they were both doing two to three more laps with me, so I went out at Steve H.'s pace. Turns out, he was just doing one lap, so he pushed it; it was not a good idea for me to stay at his pace. I felt really strong, but because of the pace, I forgot to eat and drink much, and I really paid for it on the last lap.

At this point, it was dark, the NoDoz had worn off (I thought), and I was getting very down physically, mentally, and spiritually.

Again, there's a lesson here. When it comes to my pacer, I really have to run from the front, especially during the race. I am pretty easily lulled into too fast of a pace, especially because I felt so strong, and this ended up *not* being a good idea.

Again, at this point (about 3.5 hours into the run), I was not hungry or thirsty, but I forced myself to have a snack.

Amazingly, about five minutes later, I felt awesome! Note to self again, stay fed and hydrated at *all times!*

Finished with about twenty-two miles in 4.5 hours.

Here's another funny story about the NoDoz. I was starving after the run, so on the way home, I called my wife and asked her to order me a pizza (yum). When I got home, I showered, got my feet on ice, and started eating the fantastic pizza.

At this point, it was about 11:00 p.m., and I had to get up early go camping. I figured I would just go to bed. Well, sleep was not going to happen!

Ended up staying up till 2:00 a.m.

I was up at 7:00 a.m. to go camping and had a great day and night with Ryan and the Cub Scouts. A bonus was that this campsite was so large, and we walked to so many different events. I could add a few miles to my training log on a day off.

Because of the lack of sleep Friday, I actually had the best night's sleep I have ever had on a camping trip and woke up Sunday feeling nice and refreshed. I ended the week with a strong eight-mile run down at the river; it felt effortless.

Seventy-three miles (or more, not really sure, as I estimate mileage based on time running) to cap off the most running I have ever done in a week in my life!

## *Twelve Days to Go: Taper*

It is Monday morning, and I am coming off my first of three taper weeks before my big event. The taper plan looks like this:

- Week 3: total of thirty-five miles (about 50 percent of week 4), long run no more than fifteen miles

- Week 2: total of fifty miles, long run no more than fifteen miles

    It's strange, I know, but my "coach" (in quotes 'cause I don't actually pay him; he just gives me advice here and there via e-mails and texting) and good friend, to say the least, has been doing this type of taper with his Ironman athletes, and it is working well—huge drop three weeks out, bump back up two weeks out to keep fitness high and eliminate all the funkiness (tight muscles, heavy legs, depressed and anxious Rami, etc.) that occurs with a big taper, and then virtually nothing the week of the race—just short runs to stay loose.

- Week 1: four to five runs, long run no more than eight miles and done early in week.

So the third week out, I stayed true to the program; I ran only four days—six miles, eight miles (night run), six miles, and a very fun thirteen miler with friends on Sunday. About thirty-five miles total if you include hiking around with family on Saturday.

How was I feeling? Physically, I felt great. I was still having foot pain, but it was totally manageable. Legs felt good. Body was a bit tight, but that is normal.

Mentally, I was getting a bit edgy, not so much about the training or the physical side of the race but about the logistics of a hundred-mile race!

In the next twelve days, I had to coordinate:

1. work coverage for the days I will need off because of travel and anticipating not being able to walk after the race;

2. what goes in my drop bags;

3. what I will carry during the race;

4. what my pacers will carry;

5. what my crew will have; and

6. how much pizza I have to order at mile 95 if I make it to the finish.

I felt very good spiritually. I felt very strongly that God had this situation all in his hands and would bring me whatever it is that I need on November 3 and 4.

Of course, I was praying he would bring me a wonderful day and amazing religious insights.

However, I was willing to accept and learn from whatever he decides is best for my path, even if that includes thirty hours of suffering and misery, a dreaded DNF, or fifteen hours of joy followed by fifteen hours of suffering.

Your will be done.

## *Solitude Versus Fellowship: I Want Both!*

The weekend of October 20, 2012, was a nice contrast of solo running versus running with a group.

Before, when I ran for only my own selfish reasons, I really preferred running with a group. I liked the motivation, fellowship, and the competition that occurred, as the main reason I was running was to get better at the sport I was competing in.

Now that I am developing a relationship with God through my running, I find that running solo is much more beneficial to helping me achieve my goals.

Let me use a recent run as an example. On the weekend of October 20, 2012, I was scheduled to do a 50K Fat Ass run with a local running group I do some training with.

If you remember from previous chapters, a Fat Ass run does not mean that we are all slow and overweight (although a lot of us are, myself included, some parts of the year). It means this is a mostly self-supported run (it is really a race, but they cannot call it that because they don't get any permits for it). It started at the organizer's house, where she had some food and drink, and she placed a little water out on the course. That is about it—no course markings, no T-shirts or awards at the end (except a pumpkin pie), and no fanfare.

Entry fee was $5, plus a can of food to be donated to the homeless and a pumpkin of your choice.

Pumpkin? What the heck?

Turns out there was a special prize for people who carried a pumpkin for a full lap over the top of Kennesaw mountain. I bought the smallest pumpkin I could find, but I didn't read the "race" instructions very well. Turns out it was a drawing to see which pumpkin you would carry, and some of them were pretty big!

Anyway, this race was 10K loops. If you wanted to do the whole 50K, you did five of them, about one thousand feet of climbing per loop. I decided, even before the race began, that I would only do two or three loops based on how

I felt. With only thirteen days till my first hundred miler, I didn't want to do more damage than good at that point!

So how do we compare solitude to fellowship? Let's follow my morning to see the differences. I ended up getting the best of both worlds!

### *Meeting a Friend to Drive Up to the Race With*

The upside of this is it increases the motivation to actually make the run happen (i.e, much less likely to hit the snooze or turn off the alarm if you are tired, sore, it's raining, etc.). It is also nice to have companionship to talk with on drive up and share expenses.

The downside of having a training partner(s) can be these: feeling obligated to get up at a certain time, having to accommodate someone else's stuff, energy, etc.

### *Solitude or Traveling to the Run/Race Solo*

I can go at my own schedule, my own time and energy, listen to my own music, and stop whenever I want. I don't have to think about others, and it's *much easier* to pray and be in touch with the Lord, especially on the way to races.

### *The Run Itself*

Training with a group can be a really smart thing on particularly dangerous or very primitive trails, as there is more safety in numbers if someone gets hurt.

The downside for this is when you are with a group, you feel much more obligated to go at the group's pace. This is ameliorated when the group is very large, as it invariably breaks up into smaller groups that go at a pace that is good for you. The other good thing is if you pick your training partners correctly, you can pick people that are a bit slower than you for your recovery runs and people that are a bit faster than you when you want to push yourself.

Group runs are also very smart if you are directionally challenged like myself.

On this particular day, we started out much faster than I normally do, which is not good for my warm-up period.

On the upside, I knew where I was going 'cause I could follow someone. This turned out to be very good 'cause I assumed I would always be with someone, so I didn't listen to the course instructions at all (not an uncommon occurrence for me). I ended up hanging with a group that was around my pace. A bunch of them were training for Pinhoti, so the banter was fun also.

As we crested the top of the mountain, I realized I was having some GI issues and would need to take a pit stop at the bathroom if I was going to make another lap! As we ran down the road off the mountain, I told the group I was running with I would catch up with them after I took care of much-needed business.

One of the advantages of running with experienced runners is you do not have to explain these excursions at all; everyone has been there and totally understands.

Anyway, my buddy, Troy B., told me it was about quarter mile each way to the bathroom, so I figured I would lose about ten minutes and catch them on the next lap.

I figured correctly and lost about twelve minutes, headed back out, and picked up my pace as fast as I thought was safe, as I was in taper mode and didn't want to do too much damage.

This ended up being my favorite part of the run.

I loved being solo for a while and going at my own pace. I put on some tunes and enjoyed the difference running on my own versus with a group.

I am pretty familiar with the difference, but this day gave me a direct comparison, as I did both in one run (this happens a *ton* in ultramarathon races).

I ended up catching the group on the way up the hill that I had left them on (we reversed directions each lap) and enjoyed the rest of the run with my pacer after we ended up dropping the group later in the run.

### *The Bottom Line*

Group running is good. Running with a friend is better. Running solo, especially when I need prayer and introspective time, is the best!

A typical light meal after a long run

Happy clients done with their workout at FormWell!

Not difficult for this girl, go, Hana!

I *love* waterfalls

Not something you see everyday in the
middle of the trail, only in California

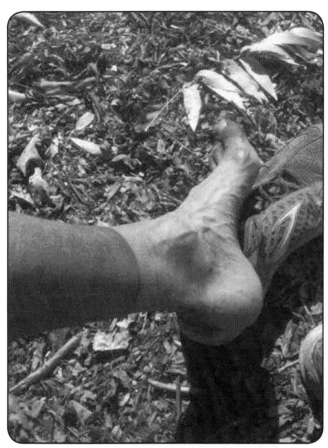

Again, only in California—never gets
this dusty on Georgia trails

Okay, this part of running in California
was pretty darn cool

Ryan and Hana helping to pack for the race

Very cold on top of Springer Mountain—Tim
does not remember this picture being taken.

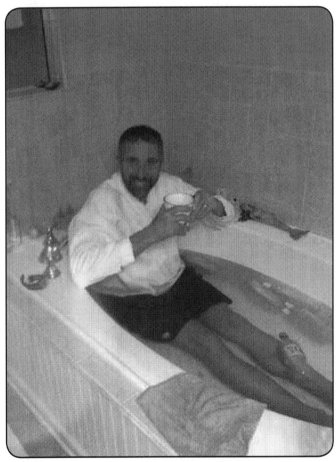

A common place to find me after long runs

A typical "small" group run with the Ultra Running crowd!

A very determined Ryan finishing his first cross-country race. Note all the 7th grade girls checking him out (I brought this to his attention).

One of the very few paved trails I enjoy: the Rails to
Trails section near where I grew up in Westchester
County, New York. This was an old railroad bed I rode
my motocross bike on when I was eleven years old!

Nothing better than finishing a run in
pouring rain with your dad!

Yes, this was a trail before a huge rainstorm in Atlanta, and, yes, I ran down this. (Fun!)

Hana at her first communion—total and complete
reverence for our Lord—no noise here!

Braves Country Fathers Day 4-Miler June 16, 2012

You have heard of the Lance-Armstrong look? This is that look in the Odeh family. (Ryan knows he has me here!)

*Random Scenes from the Race*

Such affirming and positive motivation from my crew!

*So* happy to see my family and crew for the first time
at mile 41—I didn't want to leave this aid station!

Hana and our dog Comet running out
to cheer us on at mile 52-ish.

# *The Finish!.*

Ten feet to go!

Finishing with my team!

You can stop running now!

First time sitting down in about
twenty-seven hours—relief!

## *The Day After*

Chafing from a headlamp—not expected!

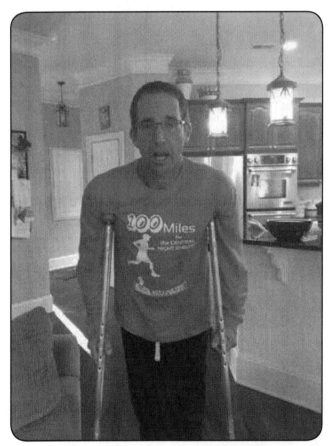

Yes, I needed these the day after.

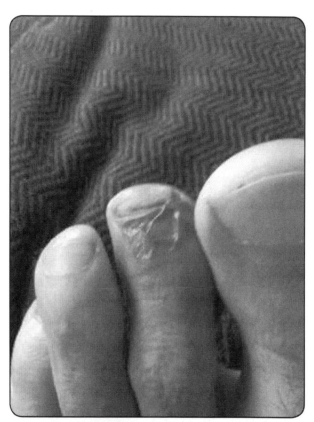

Wouldn't be one of my books without
the obligatory toe picture

Cannot get off couch but all worth it for this buckle!

# PART 3
# ONE HUNDRED MILES IN JUST OVER ONE DAY

*Let us run with endurance the race God has set before us.*

—Hebrews 12:1 (NLT)

# The Preparation

*Whatever you do, do well.*

—Ecclesiastes 9:10 (NLT)

Ah, where to start? As I said in my last book about training for my first fifty (fifty-three actually; as I have mentioned countless times, all distances in ultramarathons are *-ish*), the preparation started when I was fifteen and ran my first loop around my block.

At the time, I hated running. I didn't understand why anyone who wasn't being chased did it, and I only started because I thought it would get me in better shape for racing motocross, which it did.

Amazingly, given this inauspicious beginning, since I was fifteen, running has been one of the only constants in my life. For the next thirty-five years, running has played a small part to a very large part in my life.

The largest part, by far, was July 16–November 4, 2012 (sixteen weeks).

If you have read my other book, you know that running one hundred miles has been a goal in the back of my head ever since I got started in trail running in 2008. The stars finally aligned, and I finally found a good reason to do it in November of 2012!

My training, as I have always said, began a long time ago. Training for something like this takes years to build up to (at least for me) and then a very concerted training effort for four to eight months before.

I choose the shortest amount of time I thought would get me across the finish line—about sixteen weeks. I knew this training program would take some serious time away from the rest of my life, and I didn't want to have that stretch over eight months.

My previous chapters covered all the way until the last week of the race, so I will begin the final preparation with the final week.

The week before a big race is normally a very stressful time for me, and this one was no exception. Normally, I am worried and fretting about not training enough or all the mysterious injuries that seem to always pop up in the final weeks of a taper.

This time, the stress was all about logistics!

My body actually felt awesome. This new form of tapering (three weeks out, huge drop in volume; two weeks out, bump back up; and final week, biggest drop in volume) really worked well. My body never tightened up, and my nagging injuries almost all got much, much better!

The final week of training is really pretty funny. After all the running I have been doing, this week, I ran these distances:

- Monday–off
- Tuesday–5 miles on treadmill
- Wednesday–4 miles on treadmill, chiropractic checkup/adjustments
- Thursday–off, light massage
- Friday–2 miles on treadmill

I didn't decide this ahead of time. It just felt intuitively like the right thing to do all my runs on a treadmill, mostly because of my paranoia of turning an ankle three days out from the race on the trails!

Yep, 11 miles total for the week. Since I was praying my total for Saturday and Sunday would be 100.59 miles, I figured this was enough.

Some people don't train at all in their final week. This does not work for me, and I don't recommend it to my friends and clients. I really feel you have to keep your body loose and flowing, and your nervous system awake, before you tax it with a big effort.

The volume can be really low, but you should always throw in some pickups during your workouts (short sprints), no matter how slow you will be running your race.

It works for me, and it has worked for the people I have coached.

Anyway, as I mentioned, the physical side of the final week was fantastic and nonstressful, and I was feeling pretty darn good!

However, getting ready for a hundred-mile run with pacers, crew, and friends there to support you is not easy. Add to this fact that I picked a point-to-point race, so there was no central place people could meet up. This was a logistical nightmare.

My nervousness added to my constant OCD in the form of checking the upcoming weather daily—okay, sometimes hourly (like I could do anything about it). I used hand sanitizer constantly and avoided shaking anyone's hands. I was paranoid going up and down the stairs. I avoided social contact.

Call me the modern Howard Hughes, except without his money.

On a side note, I have always wanted to do an adventure race, and this made me think twice about it—well, at least the long ones, where you have to do everything I had to do *and* carry all your food and supplies 'cause they are not supported events (i.e., no aid stations). Not for this OCD, nervous boy!

One thing that I found helped with the anxiety was watching inspirational running videos on my computer every chance I got. I could tell I was in a pretty fragile state, as almost every one of them made my cry!

On Monday night, I wrote out a list of what I would need to carry with me, what my pacers would need, what my crew would need, and what would be in my five drop bags that were to be left out on the course by the race directors.

This list alone was an ultramarathon in itself!

Even though you really don't have to worry about nutrition because there are eighteen aid stations out on the course, you still need your own favorite things. Here is what the list looked like when I started (it changed a bit for race day, but this will give you an idea). BTW, Bubala is Bob T., Sweaty Rob is Rob S., and Goose is Troy B.

## *Planning and Logistics*

*I WILL CARRY (italics added after race):*

1. HAT AND LONG SHIRT FOR START, GLOVES–*I didn't need these, but I still wore long shirt and hat till it got light*

2. ENOUGH SALT PILLS FOR WHOLE RACE (two per hour, sixty total)

3. ENOUGH ALEVE FOR WHOLE RACE (one per eight hours, five total)–*More on this later.*

4. ENOUGH TYLENOL FOR WHOLE RACE (one per four hours, eight total)–*I forgot this.*

5. VISOR (HANG FROM BELT)

6. HYDRATION PACK

7. OLD HEADLAMP / EXTRA BATTERIES

8. IMODIUM

9. GELS (NO CAFFEINE)–*I didn't pack enough.*

10. CAFFIENE PILLS–*Label bag clearly!*

11. FACE WIPE TOWEL- *Great move!*

12. EYE DROPS–*Another great move!*

13. iPOD (FULLY CHARGED!)

*PACERS CARRY:*

1. EXTRA HEADLAMP

2. EXTRA BATTERIES

3. EXTRA MEDS

4. LONG ZIP TIES

5. SMALL FLASHLIGHT

6. HANDHELD WATER BOTTLE

7. OWN NUTRITION, SALT PILLS, MEDS, ETC.

*They didn't need any of the above, except their own water and nutrition. Realized later that "only" running thirteen to thirty-two miles (really only four to six at a time, as everything you could ever want is at every aid station) doesn't take quite as much planning on their parts!*

*MY CREW CARRIES:*

1. CAMERA–*For some reason, minimal pictures were taken. Maybe 'cause I ran so fast—not!*

2. ɪPHONE: UPDATE FACEBOOK AS OFTEN AS YOU CAN–*This was another good move as the website updates did not work this year.*

3. COMMUNICATE WITH PACERS AFTER MILE 40—WHAT DO I NEED AT WHAT AID STATION? *What did hundred-mile runners do before the invention of Facebook and iPhones?*

4. ICE-COLD DRINKS: G2, ENSURE, POWERADE ZERO, ASSORTED (REAL, NOT DIET) SODAS–*This was crucial and* much-*appreciated!*

5. SALAMI AND CHEESE SANDWICH–*I decided against this; I never tried it during a run in training. This was a good move 'cause the way my stomach felt, I would have tossed at whoever offered it to me!*

6. WATERMELON!- *This was too much work, so I decided against it. Bummer, 'cause I probably could have eaten it.*

7. OTHER SOLID FOOD IDEAS? THINK LOW FIBER, HIGH SALT, FAT, PROTEIN, CARB, AND EASY TO EAT–*This was a nonissue as no food, except soup, looked appetizing after mile 40.*

8. EXTRA HYDRATION BLADDER–*This was not needed.*

9. FIRST AID KIT–*Nothing in a first aid kit could have helped my feet!*

10. ACCELERADE: FOR LATER IN RACE, TWO SCOOPS IN HANDHELD IF NEEDED–*I forgot about this, probably would have helped.*

11. HANDHELD WATER BOTTLES (FILL WITH *ICE-COLD* DRINKS: VARY G2 AND POWERADE ZERO)–*This was a very good move!*

12. EXTRA FACE WIPE TOWEL (DIP IN ICE WATER!)–*Fantastic!*

13. SLEEPING BAG / PILLOW–*I never even sat down, so this was a nonissue also. Pillow was nice on the ride home, however!*

14. EXTRA CONTACTS, EYE STUFF, GLASSES–*I didn't need these but good to know they were there*

15. EXTRA MEDS: ALEVE, TYLENOL, IMODIUM, GINGER CHEWS, *TUMS–The only ones I needed were Tylenol and Tums, and of course, I forgot to pack both!*

16. DUCT TAPE!–*Troy B. should have carried this to tape my mouth shut as I asked him about a hundred times in thirty-two miles, "What mile are we at? What is our pace? How much time do I have in the bank for the cutoff?"*

17. DENTAL FLOSS–*I didn't need it, as just about everything I ate was liquid!*

18. FOR FINISH: COLD BEER, MEDS, CHANGE OF CLOTHES, HUGS!–*More on this later.*

*DROP BAGS/CREW INSTRUCTIONS*
*(italics added after race)*

1. MILE 27

    - MOUNTAIN DEW (DRINK!)
    - ENSURE (DRINK!)–*This was a* bad *move; more on this later*
    - PEANUT M&M'S (TAKE)
    - FIG NEWTONS (TAKE)
    - PB AND HONEY SANDWICH (TAKE)–*I made four of these and never ate one*
    - EXTRA GELS (NO CAFFEINE)

2. MILE 40 (PICK UP BUBALA)

    - FANTA (DRINK!)
    - ENSURE (DRINK!)
    - CHOCOLATE-COVERED RAISINS (TAKE)
    - PB AND HONEY SANDWICH (TAKE)
    - FIG NEWTONS (TAKE IF WANTED)
    - EXTRA LONG-SLEEVED SHIRT (TAKE)–*I actually dropped off long sleeve here; I didn't need extra.*
    - TRISLIDE *(GIVE TO PACER OR CREW)–It didn't work, at all. I wish I had a picture of my rashes, but this is a G-rated book, and they were not pretty!*
    - HANDHELD WITH ACCELERADE (TAKE)
    - HEADLAMP (TAKE)

- EXTRA HAT / GLOVES (TAKE IF NEEDED)–*There was no need at all!*
- EXTRA GELS (NO CAFFEINE)

3. MILE 55 (PICK UP SWEATY ROB AND A LARGE BAG)
   - MOUTAIN DEW (DRINK!)
   - ENSURE (DRINK!)
   - PEANUT M&M'S (TAKE)
   - PB AND HONEY SANDWICH (IF NEEDED TAKE)
   - FIG NEWTONS (TAKE IF WANTED)
   - NEW SOCKS (PUT ON IF NEEDED)–*I didn't do it; I should have.*
   - NEW SNEAKERS (CHANGE INTO)–*I didn't do it; I should have.*
   - WARM CLOTHES (LONG PANTS, JACKET, LONG SHIRT)–*I never changed socks or shoes or needed any clothes.*
   - EXTRA GELS (CAFFEINE)

4. MILE 69 (PICK UP GOOSE)
   - FANTA (DRINK!)
   - ENSURE (DRINK!)
   - CHOCOLATE-COVERED RAISINS (TAKE)
   - EXTRA GELS (CAFFEINE)
   - EXCHANGE HANDHELD FOR COLD ORANGE POWERADE ZERO

5. MILE 85
  - MOUNTAIN DEW (DRINK!)
  - ENSURE (DRINK!)
  - EXTRA GELS (MIXED)
6. MILE 95
  - GIVE HYDRATION PACK TO CREW, EXCHANGE HANDHELD FOR COLD GRAPE G2–*I forgot to do this; I should have; finish line pictures would have looked much cooler!*
7. MILE 99 OR STADIUM
  - PICK UP EVERYONE TO RUN WITH!

Once I got this list done, it was time to firm up plans for my pacers. I was having three people run with me, starting at mile 41, mile 55, and mile 68.

It is interesting; the term *pacer* really is a misnomer for someone like me, who is running a slow pace, just attempting to finish this event. True pacers are used by the leaders to make sure their pace stays at or above their goal because they have very specific time and competitive goals for the race.

For someone like me, a pacer is really more of a *companion*. I wanted to have someone I knew with me, especially when it got dark, to help me psychologically when the going got rough (ironically, the toughest time physically for me was from mile 27–35, before I met up with any of my pacers; we make our own plans, and God laughs).

Also, I am directionally challenged. Okay, I am terrible, even on the best days, so having someone with me after ten hours of running was probably a good idea!

I quickly found out that this was adding more stress to an already stressful week, so I basically decided they were all very smart adults and could handle all the timing, logistics, etc. themselves. They knew were to be at what time and what to bring. What to do with me was loosely planned, but I know from experience that this can all change on race day, so I figured we would take it as it came!

I spent Tuesday to Friday planning, packing, trying to get as much rest and sleep as possible, and trying to eat as clean as possible.

Nutritionally, for fourteen days before the race, I cut myself off completely from any form of pain killer or anti-inflammatory, any alcohol (not a big deal, I drink maybe two beers a week now), all simple sugar (except sports drinks and gels during training), and say it isn't so, *all* forms of caffeine! I am such a coffee addict that I wanted to clean my system out so the caffeine would actually work keeping me up all night running.

The toughest part was the first few days of getting up at 4:15 a.m. for work with no coffee, but it was worth it.

I thought that falling asleep while running (it really does happen in these races) and running off a cliff would not be a good end to my running career.

By the time Friday came, I was really regretting choosing a point-to-point race, just from a logistical standpoint. I wanted my whole family and multiple friends there, and it was so tough figuring out where cars would be, where people would meet, etc., especially since you cannot tell anyone exactly when I would be at each checkpoint.

From a race standpoint, the point-to-point worked well 'cause there were many times that it would have been tough to keep going if I did a loop course and got to see the finish line multiple times!

On top of the normal logistics of running one of these, I was also still working on my fund-raising efforts. I had decided to honor the Lord and give the efforts of this race to him by using it to raise money for a homeless shelter in Atlanta—the night shelter for men in downtown Atlanta. My original goal was to get up to $30 per mile for the race, so if God saw fit to let me finish the whole thing, I would be able to give the shelter $3,000.

God was showing off a bit, as he sometimes does, and as of this writing, I was at almost $100 per mile!

In addition, I had reached out to two guys in my church to design and print some shirts to raise attention and have our whole "team" stand out while we ran and they crewed. They came through, but I didn't get the shirts until Thursday night (two days before the race) and had to figure out a way to get the race shirts to my pacers and the crew shirts to everyone else.

Let's add to this. On Wednesday of race week, something happened with my phone, and I lost about 50 percent of my contacts.

For some reason, I didn't freak out about this. Maybe because of my newly found faith that everything happens for a reason?

Maybe because I had so much on my mind that this didn't add much to the pile? I just chalked it up that the really important people in my life would eventually call me, and I would have their contacts again. I also figured it was God's way of purging what does not matter in my life right now!

It all worked out.

# *The Day Before*

It's Friday, November 2, twenty-four hours before race day.

Thursday night before the race, I tried my best to be asleep by 8:30 p.m. to get a solid eight hours. I ended up going to bed at 9:30 p.m., so seven hours would have to do. I looked at the positive in that seven hours and told myself getting up at 4:15 a.m. for work would make it easier to go to bed Friday night. I knew I would be nervous and tossing and turning.

Friday, I worked a quick morning shift, got out of there at 9:00 a.m., and headed home to pack all my various bags (tried to get it done Thursday night but not enough time). It is amazing how out of it my mind gets when I am nervous and trying to plan for something like this. I don't want to overpack, but I try to think of every contingency, which I know intellectually you cannot do.

This was a nice test of my faith.

At a certain point, I just packed up what I thought I would need and then gave the rest to God. He has always provided just what I need (not what I *want* or *think* I want, but what I really *need*), and I knew he would do it for this race also!

We also made a good decision about the family logistics. Originally, I wanted them all there Friday night so we could have dinner together and experience the whole weekend as a family. Then we got to thinking about it.

Okay, my wife, the smart one in this relationship, was the one who got to thinking about this.

I wanted calm time and wanted to be in bed by 7:30 a.m. Friday night. This would be unfair to the kids and to Heather and Heather's buddy (Vikki C.), who flew in from California to help crew and be there in case one of my pacers got injured. So we decided I would go by myself and they would meet me as soon as they could get there, probably at mile 41 when I picked up my first pacer.

I immediately felt a sense of peace and knew this was the correct decision.

I am really a pain in the butt (even more than normal) with my prerace rituals, and this being the biggest race of my life, I knew I needed some alone time.

Got all packed up and headed out around 12:00 p.m. Another logistical issue was where to stay the night before the race. Most people stay at the finish line and take a bus (leaves at 4:00 a.m.) to the start. I was so intent on getting as much sleep as possible, so I decided to get a room near the start for Friday night and a room (for my family, remember, I would be running all night) near the finish for Saturday night.

I still had to drive down to the finish town to pick up my race number and drop off my drop bags, which added 1.5 hours to my drive time.

Really put things in perspective as I drove down after getting off I-20 on backroads next to the Talladega National Forest, and I thought, *This is over 1 hour in the car. I will be running through those woods all day and night tomorrow.*

Wow, scary.

When I first started driving, I was very nervous and having some serious anxiety. I turned off the music and did a full rosary, really taking my time praying between each decade.

Calm and peaceful for the rest of the trip.

After I dropped off my stuff and got my number, there was a two-hour break before the race meeting, dinner, and guest speaker. I made another on-the-spot decision to skip all that and head back to my hotel so I could have an early dinner and get to bed early. I also know that prerace meetings, hanging around expos, and talking to other racers is fun, but it normally adds to my stress.

It was time to be smart and logical.

Another good move! My intuition and, more importantly, my trust in the peace the Lord gives me when I make certain decisions were really paying off!

Drove back up (appreciating the National Forrest again, from the other side of it this time) and got to my hotel around 5:00 p.m. Original plan was to meet some friends who were doing the race at a Mellow Mushroom down the street. Fellowship and my normal prerace meal—pizza—sounded good.

Again, intuition and prayer took over.

I had passed two steak houses, and they both called to me. I also thought about being around all the other racers and that it would probably be crowded and decided to have some more alone time.

Again, God was with me. There was a steak house right across the street from my hotel! At 5:00 p.m., it was not crowded. I sat at the bar and had a wonderful prerace meal.

- One beer to calm the nerves
- Lots of ice water
- Steak with extra salt–healthy protein to help the muscle breakdown and iron for healthy blood
- Baked sweet potato with butter, cinnamon, and extra salt–nice long-lasting carbs
- Homemade mashed potatoes (suggestion from bartender—amazing) with, you guessed it, extra salt. Just a treat, as I wouldn't be having dessert.

Let me switch gears here for a minute regarding the extra salt.

There are a few reasons I picked the Pinhoti as my hundred-mile adventure. A good friend who has done it twice told me how great and what an adventure it was, it was close to home, it was not expensive, etc.

However, the main reason I picked it was the time of year.

As you know by now, I have never, ever performed at my best in the heat. The Pinhoti is held in November, and the average temperatures are low forties to low sixties, perfect running weather for me. In fact, after talking to a lot of people who had done the race, I added long pants, gloves, a hat, and an extra shirt to my drop bag at mile 55. They said that last year, it never got above fifty-five degrees, and at night, it dropped to twenty-seven at the top of one of the climbs with 30 mph winds.

Well, not this year.

I obsessively checked the weather report from ten days out, and it kept getting worse and worse (for this cold-weather runner). As the race got closer, it looked like we might actually break the Alabama record high for this day—eighty-three degrees.

Again, I was peaceful about this. Nothing I could do about it, and I knew God had his plan for this day. I would just roll with it.

I know, it sounds strange that I checked the weather obsessively *and* I claimed be peaceful, but it is the truth. I think the checking is more of a habit than a worry thing.

Or just something to do when bored.

That didn't mean I wouldn't prepare, however! Lots of good hydration the week before and lots of extra salt the few days before.

Got done with dinner around 6:00 p.m. and headed back to the room. So glad I didn't stay at the race finish late, I still had to prep my clothes for the morning, etc.

Got everything done, set three alarms *and* set a wake-up call (paranoid, maybe), and actually fell asleep before 8:00 p.m. with no problem.

Prayers before bed and thankfulness to God that I could attempt this gave me a peacefulness that overcame any racing thoughts or obsessive thinking that might have kept me up.

## *The Morning Of*

I slept solid and actually woke up at 3:30 a.m. Atlanta time (2:30 a.m. Alabama time). Believe it or not, I was so calm I went back to sleep for another hour and woke up *before* any of the alarms (they were set for 3:30, 3:40, and 3:45 a.m., and the wake-up call was set for 3:30 a.m.)!

The race start was 6:00 a.m., and my hotel was only twelve miles from the start, so originally, I was going to get up at 4:00 a.m. and leave the hotel at 5:00 a.m. to allow plenty of time to get there and get settled in.

However, the night before, God stepped in and caused a conversation with another racer who had scouted out the start that day. Turns out the last seven miles to the start were all on fire roads—very dusty and very slow; he said to allow forty-five minutes just to get there. That and we had to park about a half mile from the start, so I planned on leaving at 4:30 a.m. to be safe.

Another in a long series of God-inspired good moves on the day.

Right out of bed, I took a long, hot shower. I then had my prerace meal (prepped at home the day before).

- Pasta with butter, olive oil, and lots of salt
- Four scrambled eggs with butter and...well, you know by now
- G2 for drink
- Planned on a banana also but was too full.

Got all lubed up (I knew no matter what I did, chafing would be an issue, but I wanted to avoid it as much as possible), dressed, and did some foam-roller work.

Got downstairs around 4:45 a.m., which still gave me an hour and fifteen minutes to get to the start line twelve miles away. Normally, I get to races almost an hour before they start, especially ones this important, but the race director said that since they have to wait till the buses arrive before they can start, no one is usually there till 5:30 a.m.

I tried to push my luck on the intuition and God inspiration and stay relaxed and in the moment and asked some friends if they knew how to get to the start. I figured if I could just follow them instead of a map, I could relax, pray, listen to tunes, and get in race mode.

They said they did.

But they didn't

We took two wrong turns that added about ten minutes to the drive. The drive on the dirt road was miserable. It hadn't rained here in a long time, and it was so dusty you couldn't see ten feet in front of you.

Finally get to the area where we can park—it is even farther away from the start than I thought—at around 5:40 a.m. Another logistical issue is I had to leave my car here, and Heather had to come get it so it would be at the finish (all my postrace stuff was in the car, and we would need it to get everyone home).

# THE RACE!

*Anything is possible if a person believes.*

—Mark 9:23 (NLT)

Walked down to the start line and arrived at 5:52 a.m., eight minutes to spare. Not a recipe for a calm race start, but with God by my side, I was calm and happy as could be.

To digress a bit, another very cool and wonderful thing that had happened through our church is that the head of the church—Monsignor F.—started training with me at our gym. He has had fantastic results and has been such a blessing to have in my life. He constantly is thanking me for how much better he looks and feels, and I am constantly thanking him for being such a wonderful client and religious mentor in my life.

It is a pretty cool relationship.

Anyway, he is actually part of the reason I chose the night shelter to raise money for. I met with him to discuss it about a year before the race because I wanted to know which Catholic charity he thought could most benefit from the cash I would raise. We then both came up with the idea of doing the night shelter, as it is a mission that our church and church men's club help out with. Also, it is small and would really benefit from 100 percent of the funds going directly to them—no admin costs coming out on my end!

As we trained and talked about my race, he started talking about coming to the start of the race to give me a blessing and send me on my way with God's grace, strength, and protection.

I was floored he would even think about this. The race start was 2.5 hours away from Atlanta, it started at 6:00 a.m. on a Saturday, and he is an extremely busy priest.

But he was serious.

So I e-mailed the race director and told him he was coming and he would do a quick blessing for any athletes who were interested. The director thought it was a cool idea, and the monsignor planned on getting there at 5:30 a.m., as did I.

None of us knew the road situation until it was too late to let him know. I called him at about 5:15 a.m., when I realized it was going to be slow going on his way down, but he didn't get the message in time.

So back to race start, I am peaceful and calm but a little disappointed that the monsignor is not there, and I also feel very bad that he did this for me, and I didn't get down there on time.

I did my best to trust the Lord that it was all the way it should be, said some quick private prayers, and lined up to start.

Turns out there were many, many racers who got held up by the road and parking situation. We saw them running down the road as we started the race (you had to sign in before you started, or you would be disqualified; I actually talked to one guy who started at 6:20 a.m.!).

There were 240 people who signed up for the race, 192 started (20 percent did not start rate), and only 108 finished (56 percent of starters finished, 45 percent of total signed up finished).

It was really cool starting in the dark, running from this isolated start area in the woods to a small high school stadium one hundred miles away.

Really cool and a bit crazy.

But what was *really* cool was what happened next.

I am about a hundred feet into the race—started myself about in the middle 'cause I estimated, based on previous races, that that is the pace I would be holding. I am looking around, frantically hoping to see the monsignor, when, all of a sudden, I hear this person with a strong Irish accent yelling, "Rami! Rami! Rami!"

I run over to the side, and there is Monsignor F. with his Bible, a *huge* flashlight, and wearing the bright orange "100 Miles for the Night Shelter" T-shirt I gave him! He gives me a big hug and apologizes for being late. Imagine that, him apologizing to me! I felt so bad he had driven all that way and not made the start.

We were both apologizing profusely and hugging and then I think we both realized that there was still a race going on!

He gave me a wonderful, albeit a bit rushed and out-of-breath, blessing for God to be with me the whole way, protect me, and give me the strength I would need to finish. I have him another hug, told him I loved him, and was back in the race.

What an amazing way to start. Had I not been late, I might not have started where I did. I might not have been where I was in the crowd, and I might have missed him.

God's plan really is incredible.

When you quiet your mind enough to hear and see it.

## *Miles 1–27*

Because of my unplanned stop for my wonderful blessing, I ended up back with the end of the race. Most people back here were walking to start. Not a big deal. There was no need to start out fast, but I had heard that if you didn't get close to the front in this race, you would lose a lot of time in the first few miles with bottlenecks at stream crossings, etc.

Most trail races have about a mile of road or jeep road at the start to allow things to open up a bit before the race goes to single track.

Not the Pinhoti 100.

We were only on the road for about two hundred feet before we turned off onto the trail!

So here is a funny sight. There were two hundred people who trained their butts off to run this race, and about a hundred of them were just standing in line after the race starts to get on the trail. I, again, gave it to God and had trust that he had it all in his loving hands. Figured having the monsignor there late was his way of slowing me down, getting me behind the bottleneck, and keeping my pace down at the start of the race.

I figured correctly.

The first mile was basically a fast walk or very slow jog until things started to open up a bit. At one point, we had to wait in line for the only way to cross a stream without getting wet. We waited for a pretty long time. Some people couldn't take it and ran through the water. I had a feeling how bad the blisters would be even without wet shoes and socks, so I waited.

The beginning of this course was absolutely perfect running trails. No big hills, very nontechnical terrain, and soft surface. The exact opposite of the first ten miles of the Georgia Jewel 50, which destroyed my feet six weeks before this one. Even though it was dark for the first forty-five minutes, you could see the beauty of this trail with all the headlamps. It was fantastic!

The ease of the terrain in the beginning of this course could have put a real damper on my race, as it would have been really tempting to go out fast. But I was blessed to have my "monsignor moment" slow me down, so I was held back for at least the first hour of the race.

In fact, I was actually joking with some other racers that we might all be pulled from the race at the first aid station 'cause we didn't make the time cutoff for the thirty-hour limit!

I carried with me a chart of each aid station that showed what time you had to be there to be at a twenty-four-hour pace and thirty-hour pace (it also showed the fifteen-hour-pace, which is around what the winners would do, not a worry for me).

The first aid station was at 6.7 miles, and the time cutoff for a thirty-hour pace was two hours. We barely made it!

The beginning of these long races is always my favorite part. My body feels fantastic, my stomach is perfect, and everyone is in a really talkative, fun mood. I said to myself and other runners, more than once, that I really want to come back to this trail to train and do some shorter runs so I could actually run at my normal pace without worrying about finishing 100 miles!

The first marathon (that sounds pretty crazy, doesn't it?) was pretty uneventful. The trail was beautiful, the sunrise was majestic, and I was feeling blessed and happy to be out there. Once it opened up a bit, I picked up my pace but stayed comfortable and within myself, power walking almost every hill, even though, physically, I knew I could run them. I had never run 100 miles, but I know from my 50s that these races (at my level) are not about speed or aerobic capacity; they are about strength, perseverance, being smart, being able to hold down calories, and energy conservation.

Okay, *now* let's talk about the weather. Remember, I picked this race because historically it has had perfect running temps, especially for me.

Not this day.

It was warming up quickly. It was already up to about fifty at the start. I had a hat and a long-sleeved shirt on, but I took them off after about five miles. It was fun having that long-sleeved shirt around my midsection for thirty-five miles until I could give it to my crew!

I knew from prior experience that I would need to hydrate and eat as much as possible early 'cause my digestive system tends to shut down after about six hours running, especially when it is hot. I fueled well at every aid station and drank over 140 ounces of water in the first twenty miles!

Also, I was on a regular schedule of anti-inflammatories (Advil and Aleve) to help with inflammation (duh) and pain management, and I was taking two electrolyte pills on the hour.

After about four hours, I realized my ultrabrain would not being doing math very well (converting the stopwatch time on my watch to actual time of day), so I switched to time of day to see how my pacing was going at each aid station.

I made back all the time I lost in the first seven miles by the twenty-two-mile point and was tracking pretty close to the twenty-four-hour pace. My plan (if such a thing exists for a first-time race at this distance) was to go out a the twenty-four-hour pace for the first fifty miles, which would put three hours in the "bank" to make the thirty-hour cutoff.

My main goal for this race was to finish in under thirty hours and not permanently hurt myself in the process. I also knew that I would find out a lot about myself, my dedication and drive, and most importantly, my connection to God.

I didn't want to do anything (within my power) to jeopardize my chances of making to the finish line.

However, I will not lie. I was feeling so superfantastic in the first five hours before it got hot that I flirted with the possibility of breaking twenty-four hours.

That feeling went away after mile 27.

## *Miles 27–34*

The aid station at mile 27 was pretty cool (not temperaturewise; it was about noon at this point, and it was very, very warm). It was actually an out-and-back-up-a-rock climb next to a lake. This was the first place we could get to our drop bags.

I put soda and Ensure in each of my drop bags—soda 'cause I crave it in every long run and Ensure for easily digestible calories.

This was a great plan when the projected high temp was sixty degrees, not so much when it would now go over eighty degrees (it actually ended up tying the all-time record of eighty-three for that day in Alabama).

I also knew from talking to the other runners that the mileage between mile 27 and 34 was wrong, and instead of the 6.7 miles listed, it was closer to 8 miles.

Those 8 miles might not sound like a lot when you are running 100, but in this type of heat and at the slow pace you run, it can be well over two hours without any kind of aid. Everyone said, "Stock up at mile 27 'cause it will be a while before you get food or water again."

So I did.

Remember what I said about using Ensure during training? Well, I neglected to mention that in training, I always left them on ice in a cooler.

This day, I left my Ensure in a bag.

Sitting in the sun.

In eighty-degree weather.

I chugged down a hot—and I mean *hot*—Ensure, ate some salted potatoes, drank a bunch of Coke, and anything else that looked good.

Not a good idea.

I felt okay leaving the aid station, but after about five minutes, I started to feel really sick. I mean ready-to-puke sick. This was a quick learning experience not to eat too much in one moment and to walk for a while after leaving an aid station to digest food.

It really didn't get any better. In fact, there were many times when I thought if my stomach didn't get better, I might not be able to finish this race.

Not feeling like eating or drinking anything when you are only a fourth of the way done with a hundred miler is not a recipe for success.

I prayed a lot during this stretch and took my pace down significantly.

Thoughts of a twenty-four-hour finish—as crazy, stupid, and fleeting as they were—never, ever entered my mind again. I was back to original game plan of conserving energy and doing whatever it took to make it to the finish line.

When I finally got to the mile 34 aid station, I was actually feeling a lot better. I saw some friends and a bunch of other people at this aid station who felt like I did and looked a lot worse. Everyone was getting dehydrated and sick, and I found out later that a lot of people never left this aid station.

It was a popular place to drop out.

A woman offered me a chair to sit down in (I lovingly referred to her as Satan throughout the race), and I politely declined. I didn't know what I would feel like in the middle of the night, but I was sticking to my plan of never, ever sitting down until I crossed the finish line.

I was afraid I would never get up. I ate (much lighter this time), drank what I could, and moved on, as quickly as I could. Turns out that I was spending a lot less time at the aid stations than most people, which I think really helped me bank time in the first fifty miles.

Another funny thing happened in this stretch. All through the beginning of the race, most of us were very, very careful about taking our time over water crossings to not get our shoes and socks wet.

At one point, I actually said to myself, "I don't think I will need to change shoes at mile 55." This is where it was suggested to leave an extra pair of shoes and socks due to the large water crossing right before this aid station, and you can guess what happened next.

We come up on a stream crossing that was so high that there was no way to get across (trust me, I looked for a while) without getting wet.

Again, theme of the day, this was a blessing. The stream was very cold and just below the knee high. It cooled off my feet and ankles and relieved a lot of hot spots that were forming on the bottom of my feet. I knew it would add to the blisters later, but the immediate relief was wonderful. I also stuck my head in the water and doused my body with ice-cold stream water.

Fantastic feeling. Gave me a new start on the day.

## *Miles 34–41*

This stretch was one of my favorites in the race. My stomach felt much better, I was handling the heat better, and I could start to think about seeing my family, pacers, and crew at mile 41! One of the psychological games I set up with myself before this race was to think of it not as a hundred-mile race but as a jog or fast hike from aid station to aid station.

This was a lot easier to think of than, "Wow, I just ran twenty miles. I only have eighty to go!"

Since the aid stations were between four and eight miles apart, that meant I had something different and exciting to look forward to (especially when my family, friends, and pacers would be there) every one to two hours.

Another thing that someone said before the race that resonated with me was this old adage: "How do you eat an elephant? One bite at a time."

This actually became funny with another runner as we tried to figure our where we were in the elephant's body (i.e., ten miles in, we had barely eaten one of his feet, etc.). It got kind of gross at other parts of his body, but those are things that are only funny—and even then, only marginally so—during an ultra!

Anyway, mile 34–41 also included the climb to the highest point in the race, also the highest point in Alabama, which is about 2,700 feet. It's not very high by mountain standards, but it's a pretty decent climb up to the top. My body was performing very well at this point; all the mountain training I had done had really prepared my legs well for these types of climbs.

Actually, from a technical and elevation standpoint, this course, overall, was much easier than I expected. However, one hundred miles is one hundred miles, no matter how you slice it (or eat it).

Met up with a great group of guys on this climb—some veterans and some first timers—and we shared some humor and stories on the way up. It was really the nicest and easiest part of the race for me.

When we got to the top, we stopped to enjoy the view (it was amazing, such a clear day), and they actually took a picture of us. I've no idea who the guys were, so I will probably never see it, but it was a very cool moment. Then we hit the boardwalk that led to the aid station, and I took off.

Knowing I would see my family and friends for the first time in almost ten hours of running helped me run down the boardwalk with legs that felt as fresh as the morning!

Postscript: to give you an idea of how nice it is to see your family when you are out in the woods running for so long, as I was sitting here editing this book, almost a year after I completed the race, I started to cry when I read this section!

I had told a friend from a running group that I was going to mess with my family and limp into the station like I was hurt, but I forgot all about it when I saw them. I did look at them funny and say, "Who are all you people in orange shirts and what are you doing here?"

They didn't think it was very funny.

They were awesome! They were happy, enthusiastic, asking me what I needed, motivational, and had some great—of course, orange—signs. One of them—and I am glad it was my wife holding it, not one of my pacers—read, "I don't do ultramarathons, but I do an ultramarathoner."

Another one read, "I am glad you are only running 100.59 miles, 'cause 101 miles would just be crazy."

My kids and our friend, Vikki, made some awesome ones too. It really is amazing how wonderful it is to have a crew; I don't know how people do these races without one!

Now the frenzy began! Aid stations, when you have a large crew, are a bit like NASCAR pit stops, although not quite as fast. My goal from the beginning was to not spend a lot of time in aid stations and, as I mentioned, never, ever sit down.

Hugged my family and friends, got all fueled up, picked up my headlamp, and finally dropped off the long-sleeved shirt I had been carrying for ten hours. At this point, I was digesting food a little better but still only wanted mostly liquids. I basically resigned myself at this point that I would be in and out of nausea all day and night.

Par for the course, as they say.

I picked up my fist pacer, Bob T., aka Bubala, and we headed down the road.

## *Miles 41–55*

This section was the first major change, at least psychologically, in the race. Up until this point, I had done a mixture of solo running while enjoying music, talking with new friends while running on the trail, or a mixture of the two (taking one earbud out so I could hear the other runner and still have some music in the background). Some of the conversations were cool, some I walked away from, some I tuned out of, but none of them were personal.

Now I had a very good friend to hang with for the next four hours.

That made me happy!

Bob and I started our run down the mountain road that leads to the park at the top of Mount Cheaha. This was nice, as it gave Bob a chance to warm up and me a chance to stretch out my legs after the long climb up and the break at the aid station. We then turned off the trail onto what is affectionately known as Blue Hell. This is a steep—very steep—downhill that is mostly large boulders, loose rocks, and big gnarly roots.

Fun!

I was actually having a good time, talking to Bob about everything that had happened up to that point and having fun basically climbing down this section. I slipped a couple of times and took what would end up being my only "fall" of the race. It is in quotes because I was sliding down a very steep, slippery section, and I fell back on my butt; however, it was so steep that the distance between my butt and the ground was very, very small.

Bob and I agreed it couldn't technically be called a fall. I laughed, he laughed, and we moved on.

Again, this section was tough but not nearly as tough as described by other racers who had done this race before.

This really became the theme, at least in my head (I didn't want to vocalize it 'cause every time I do that, it seems something brutal shows up within five minutes)— the topography and technicality of this trail was really easy compared to what I had been training and racing on for the past six months! I kept telling people how much I loved the trail and how much fun it was.

People who had not trained on technical, rocky mountains like I had were *not* amused.

I really enjoy running with Bob T., as he is one of my only running buddies who is not really into running.

Does that make sense?

Most of the people I train with train as much as me, if not more. All of them race more than me. Bob runs for exercise and to spend time with friends.

He is also a freak of nature. He can go out—and he has done this—and run fifteen miles without training and with no water or gels. He has a stronger mind than almost anyone I know.

And he is *almost* as funny, good-looking, intelligent, and humble as me, so we get along great.

So running with Bob is fun because we rarely talk about running.

Don't get me wrong. I like talking about running, but for the past ten hours, everyone I talked to talked 90 percent about running, or races, or terrain, or running shoes, or nutrition, or socks, or chafing issues, or how bad they felt, etc.

Bob and I joke the whole time and have fun with other people, and our conversations range from world politics, to religion, to marriage, to raising kids, to sports, back to religion, then a little about exercise, running, and weight loss, and then back to religion, etc.

This run was no different. We met people along the way and kept up a pretty good pace, and the only issues I was having were the pain in my feet starting to really escalate and the constant nausea, especially after I would eat anything (except chicken soup).

When the sun set, it was time to put on the headlamps and concentrate a bit more. We ran behind a few people, and this slowed our pace a bit, which was good for a while, but my legs were still feeling good, and I still wanted to bank time in case the wheels fell off later in the race. So we jumped ahead.

We got to see my family and crew at the next aid station (mile 52), and it was awesome. My daughter, Hana, actually ran out about four hundred yards with our little dog and ran with us to the station.

What a trooper.

At the last aid station before I picked up my next pacer, a guy asked if he could run with us 'cause he didn't have a headlamp. Turns out this was his first one hundred, and he thought he would make it to mile 55 before he needed it. Man, that guy must have thought he was fast. Anyway, we said sure, and he was awesome!

Either he had the same sense of humor (bad, irreverent, not really that funny except to us) that we did, or he was just going along because without us he would be out in the woods, in the dark, with no light.

It was a match made in heaven.

Really.

His name was Mike, and he ran between us to get the most light. I cannot imagine how hard that was and how much energy it took. He said he had to look ahead at my lamp and then try to guess when the root that he saw one second before would show up.

Yes, he tripped and almost fell a lot.

In fact, when the conversation turned to chafing, as it seemed to do a lot after mile 40, the ongoing joke became, "If Mike trips or falls more than thirteen times, he has to put Vaseline on Rami's butt at the next aid station."

We were kidding, of course.

That was Bob's job.

He was a real sport and went along with it. In fact, you should have heard him when he hit twelve trips. He as adamant about the fact that his next trip or fall (the Vaseline fall) had to be an all-out fall—hands flying out, at least one hand touching the ground—before it counted.

He was scared.

He ended up tripping and/or falling twenty-one times in that stretch. He is now my hero, and I am sure he has his own version of this story that is very different than ours. Probably something along the lines of, "I met this really nice gay couple named Rami and Bob from Atlanta and..."

I really don't remember much in the way of details about my section with Bob, except that, in great contrast to later in the race, the time really flew. We were both having fun, and Bob actually said he would have loved to run longer with me. It felt like one of our normal runs, except I was a bit more tired, much sicker, and not quite as funny as normal.

One last thing, the only real job I gave Bob was to remind me on the hour to take salt pills.

He never remembered to do this.

Not once.

Luckily for him and me, I was still very lucid and aware of time at this point, so I kept taking them.

Our time together came to an end, and it was time to pick up Rob, aka Sweaty Rob.

## *Miles 55–69*

Sweaty Rob, nicknamed that, well, because he sweats a lot, is a training buddy who was quickly becoming a good friend.

I figured pacing me at night for fourteen miles would either move our friendship along nicely or end it altogether.

He is an amazing athlete. His specialty is XTERRA (off-road) short-course triathlons, mountain biking, and trail running. In just two years in the sport, he actually qualified for the XTERRA national championship—twice!

On a side note, in 2013, he qualified for the world championship!

Honestly, I was most worried about him being able to handle my slow pace for so long.

Worries were not needed; he did awesome!

Rob is also a big conversationalist, but he is very different than Bob. He is married with no kids, works for the state government (Bob is a radiologist, BTW), and owns a second home up in Blue Ridge, Georgia, where he spends a lot of time training and chilling.

We talk a lot about training, and that didn't change on this run.

One of the things I learned early on with pacers is this: they are there to help me, and I can tell them to do whatever I want, within reason. This was a very different situation for me as I am normally very self-reliant on runs (and in most things in life). It was very important to tell them how I was feeling, what my plan was, etc., so they knew what to do.

With Rob, I wanted a few more things than just salt (which, remember, Bob failed miserably at).

1. Remind me to take salt on the hour.

2. Make sure I am drinking, eating, and peeing regularly.

3. Let me know our pace.

4. Unless I am really sick, make sure I run all the flats and downhills and walk all the uphills; I still wanted to bank time if I could.

5. Let me know the *grade* we were running on (this was not planned). His watch could do this, and it was very helpful. It was night, and we ran a fair bit on fire roads. It was hard to tell at some points if it was flat, downhill, or uphill!

Rob was on top of everything. In fact, he helped me make one of the most crucial physical decisions of the race. I had taken two Advil when I woke up and was taking one

Aleve every six hours to reduce inflammation and pain. This had worked well for me in my past long races, but this time, I was having some problems, one that could become serious.

First, I think they really added to my stomach problems. It's not a huge problem. I could deal with the nausea, but it could cause some serious problems later on if I started puking and not being able to replace nutrients.

The more serious problem was it was hot, and I was drinking a fair amount, taking salt, and I stopped peeing.

Not good.

We both decided the excessive anti-inflammatories (pretty sure I took some Advil at at least two aid stations on top of my regular schedule) was messing with my kidneys and reducing my ability to process my liquids.

I stopped taking them at that point.

To be honest, I don't have a lot of very clear memories of my time with Rob. I think my dehydration and stomach problems were limiting the amount of glucose to my brain, so it wasn't working very well. I also think that the intensity of pain in my feet and legs was getting so high that my mind was starting to block things out.

I do know that we ran well together, and he got me to stop once, turn off my headlamp (this is how crazy you get; he asked me to do it one time before, and I didn't want to look up 'cause I thought it would expend too much energy!), and look at the stars. They were amazing.

Rob is also fantastic at directions, estimating distance, etc., so he was a wealth of information regarding how fast we were going, how far the next aid station was, how far ahead of the cutoffs we were. This was very, very important to me and got more important as the night went on.

I do remember us encountering a guy who was really ready to drop, very down, and physically just dead. Rob spent a lot of time with him trying to get him to continue. It was amazing. This sparked a pretty long conversation about how desolate it is in these races and what would happen if you were out here without a pacer and got hurt. It would be a very long time before anyone knew, that is for sure.

I also remember telling him if he slipped and got hurt, unless he was dying, I would leave his ass out there and keep going!

I was getting pretty focused on finishing at this point.

Rob delivered me safely to my third and final pacer, Troy M. or, as I decided to affectionately call him for the weekend, Goose (think *Top Gun*).

Postscript: I'm crying again while editing this section and thinking of what good friends these guys are.

## *Miles 69–95*

Of the three pacers, Troy definitely had it the worst.

With Bob, I was still relatively fresh and happy.

With Rob, I was okay, still talking and not too bad.

Troy got the worst shift and definitely the worst version of Rami.

I think we got to him at around 11:00 p.m. The poor guy had been up all day, waiting to start running (he told me later he actually woke up at 4:30 a.m., ready to go, and couldn't go back to sleep).

Imagine waiting all day for this, and having to stay up all night nursing a hurting, obnoxious, and very nontalkative runner.

Not most people's idea of a fun Saturday night.

So he picks me up at mile 69 after waiting all day to run, and we start to…walk.

I had to let him know that after every aid station, I have to walk a while to digest what little food I could take in at this point.

We finally did start running, not fast, but fast enough to stay ahead of the cutoffs, which was all I cared about at this point.

About four miles into our run together, we started the climb up to Pinnacle, which everyone says is the hardest climb and hardest part of the race.

Of course, in typical Rami fashion, I actually enjoyed this climb. Again, it was not as hard as what I had been training on, and I didn't feel bad not running because it was steep enough to warrant a power walk. I knew we slowed down our pace, and I think this is where I started obsessively asking Troy what our pace was.

For the next ten hours, every ten minutes, or less, this is what our conversation would turn to:

Rami: "What is our pace?"

Troy: "Averaging X minutes per mile since I started with you."

Rami: "No, Troy, what is our pace right now?"

(I always wanted this to be under eighteen minutes per mile, which was the cutoff pace for a thirty-hour race)

Troy: "We are at X minutes per mile right now."

Rami: "So how far ahead of the cutoff are we?"

Troy: "You have only given back thirty-two seconds since the last time you asked me."

Rami: "What the hell does that mean? Tell me how many hours and minutes *exactly* I have in the bank."

Troy: "You are still over 3 hours ahead of the cutoff."

Rami: "Thank you. Sorry I am being such a pain."

(Okay, I didn't say this every time, but I did think it—a lot.)

It is amazing how important pacing became to me and how unrealistic my mind was becoming. If I gave back even a minute of time, even when I was 3.5 hours ahead of the cutoff time, I would pick up my pace or take less time peeing or in the aid station, etc., to make up for it.

I was *so* paranoid about not finishing. I wanted to make sure I had maximum time in the bank in case I completely fell apart in the last miles.

This is only one facet of the new "anti-Rami" that came out with Troy.

Here are more "anti-Rami" traits that surfaced after seventy miles of continuous forward movement:

- I normally love single track and hate jeep roads and regular roads, but not now; single track scared me 'cause I was so paranoid about falling and ruining my race.

- I normally love downhills; now I hated them 'cause I felt so bad walking down them.

- I normally love food; I hated everything put in front of me, except soup.

- I normally love running in the cold. When it got cold at about 4:00 a.m., I hated it.

- I never care about distance and pace anymore; with Troy, that is about *all* I cared about.

Troy also made a good point after the race; being with me for those ten hours was really like being with an infant. He had to convince me to eat and drink, I asked the same questions over and over, I was temperamental, and...I really, truly, had diaper rash.

Another thing that Rob and Troy had to do was carry my TRISLIDE, a form of spray body lube that was supposed to help alleviate the chafing issues.

It didn't work.

But it did cause a bunch of good jokes and laughs every time I would ask for it and spray it down my pants!

Another thing that was infant-esque was how proud I was and happy I was every time I peed. Remember that I stopped taking Aleve and Advil when I stopped peeing? Well, a combination of that, the cooler weather, and some caffeine pills (BTW, I didn't need anywhere near as much of this as I thought I would; the excruciating pain in my legs and feet was more than enough to keep me awake), and I started peeing regularly after about mile 75.

I found myself relying more and more on psychological help from Troy.

I also made him my personal unpaid assistant, as I would have him remind me to take salt on the hour, remind me to drink (didn't want to), remind me to eat (*really* didn't want to), tell me when I went off trail (many, many times), and best of all, carry my used food wrappers (I didn't want the extra weight; that tells you how crazy I got!).

After we made it up Pinnacle, I got to see some friends from the running group I belong to. I was looking forward to this aid station all day, as it was at the top of the worst climb, and it was basically downhill, small climbs, and flat to the finish. Also, they have some of the best food on the course—homemade soup, fried egg sandwiches, and grilled cheese.

Guess what?

I didn't want any food, and I was done running at this point, so I wouldn't get to enjoy any of the wonderful food!

Something major shifted inside me after mile 75.

Did you read above? I was *done* running!

I think I did the math in my head and realized I could power walk from there to the finish and still make the cutoffs. I was so tired and hurting. I thought that if I started running, I might use what little energy I had left and not make it.

Looking back, this was not true, but you just have no idea how weird your mind gets after all that running.

I don't think I vocalized it, or even realized it at the time, but Troy and I were about to walk over a marathon together.

Luckily, I can walk pretty fast, and I had done a lot of hill power walk training on the treadmill, so I could average as low as fifteen and sometimes fourteen-minute miles while walking, so this would get us there!

I really don't remember all that much about the rest of the night except that our world got smaller and smaller and time started to really slow down.

For both of us.

There were times when I felt like we went hours without saying a word to each other, except for my incessant questions about pacing and the cutoffs.

What I do remember is life, and my thought process, getting very, very simple, and singularly focused. Little moments of joy held paramount importance to me. Seeing the lights of the next aid station, taking a good pee, putting eye drops in when my eyes got dry, a cold towel on my face, seeing the red flags that signified we were still on the course—these things kept me going!

I also remember becoming like a *robot*, where my only function and goal in life was to keep forward momentum.

In fact, my body basically only functioned fairly well while moving. Anytime I would stop, I would get lightheaded, dizzy, and sick to my stomach.

Moving was the only option.

Because of my lack of memory, I will share Troy's wonderful write up of the final thirty-one miles here. Enjoy!

## *Troy's Write-Up: Mile 68.8 to Finish*

Rami is my new hero. One hundred miles of very tough racing in twenty-six hours, fifty-two minutes. Found on Twitter, Denise Bourassa, coming off Horn Mountain to Bulls Gap (85mi) says, "This race is *much* harder than Western States."

That about sums it up. For us southeasterners, the trail was typical rocks, roots, creeks, twists, and turns. Western trails are much more groomed, so the footing is much easier. I turned my ankles no less than four times, and Rami for sure did it more.

This is longer than normal, but this race is, well, longer than normal. For some odd reason, I awoke Saturday morning at 4:30 a.m. and could not go back to sleep. I must have been eager to do something. So I texted Rami and said good luck. I told him to start slow and back off. Rami was in a fantastic mood and ready to go.

Now, with nothing else to do, I started packing and getting ready. Meanwhile, Rami leaves the hotel with over an hour to go to the race start, which was not an hour away.

Traffic confusion and directions caused him to get there about eight minutes before the race. No time for anxiety to set in. He took solace in the fact that he wasn't the only one, and we later learned some people started way past 6:00 a.m.

Rami is a beast. Ultralive was an ultradead website, so our first updates came when Bob met up with Rami at Bald Rock at mile 40.94. He was looking great and had reasonably survived the heat of the day. Rob S. and I had set up at Adams Gap, mile 55.34, at about 3:00 p.m. to await the arrival. Adams Gap aid station was the Woodstock of ultrarunning aid stations—grills, music, tons of people, and a serious yet happy and upbeat vibe as we all waited for our runners. We were Cheering each one, and yes, there was cowbell.

The twenty-four-hour pace at Adams Gap was to arrive at 7:12 p.m. Rami rolled in 7:19 p.m. He looked fantastic. Bob said there were no problems except some poor dude didn't have a headlamp for the last section and that he ran in between Rami and Bob for light but still fell twenty-one times; Bob counted. Rami was in business mode. Selected the things he needed quickly and headed out with Rob S.

Then I went into business mode. Rami was hauling ass, and I needed to get to mile 68, change clothes, fuel ,up and try and relax. Porter's Gap aid station was not Woodstock. Mile 68 headed to a tough climb was all business. The runners were more spread out now, and crews only showed up sporadically. The only thing I really wanted was some coffee. I had a five-hour energy but decided I shouldn't do something I've never done right before I was going to pace Rami for thirty-two miles. I needed to take care of him, so I left the aid station, which had no coffee, in search of coffee. I was told Talladega was nine miles down the road. I didn't want to go that far. I stopped at the first place which, at 8:12 p.m., was closing! All three workers were smoking and watching the AL/LSU game. They had no coffee, and by their attitude, I wasn't going to get any. I left and stopped at the next place, which us pacers quickly dubbed the barred mini-mart. It looked better-suited to be on 8 mile in Detroit, not rural Alabama. They also had no coffee, and I ended up with warm, foamy, machine-provided cappuccino, *ugh*.

Okay, enough about me. I got back rested, and the crew showed up (Rami's wife, children, dog, and a friend named Vickie), so I changed. At least Rami and I would have shared the same sleep schedule. Scott, the night crew, also showed up. We started discussing where and when we would see him and what I anticipated we would need. The next two aid stations were so remote that he wouldn't be there. The next time we'd see him was mile 85. At this point, based on updates, Rami had wisely slowed down a bit. Bursting out the darkness, runners would appear. We'd run up to make sure it wasn't our runner, and we'd sit back down. Rami comes blowing into the aid station about 11:00. To be honest, it was a blur. As the crew got him what he needed, I took off the long sleeves, threw on my Camelbak, and took the hand-off from Rob. A can of TRISLIDE and a handheld water bottle for Rami. Fortunately, all I had to do was carry the TRISLIDE. Rami applied it himself.

Game time! We walked out of the aid station. Rami gave me updates on his health, his diet needs, and any issues he'd been having. Rami was about twenty-five to thirty-five minutes off a twenty-four-hour race. I told him that he had this thing in the bag. We don't need to do anything crazy to get home. Rami found solace in doing the pace math, not as much about how fast he was going but how long he had to make it home. We discussed he had over twelve hours to make it 31.81. We both thought the best climb started right out of the gate, but it didn't. We trotted through the forest, reveling in the clear star-laden skies, with a bright moon rising. We also discussed the odd fact that the temps were unseasonably warm, the cool spots were low, and the warm spots were high. On the ridges, the wind was actually warm, too warm for the likes of Rami and I. Our long-sleeved shirts tied around our waists, awaiting use that never came. I quickly settled into my job, keeping track of food, salt, hydration, pace, and trail spotting! Trail spotting became a sport. Looking for little glowing reflective flags with a headlamp was of number 1 importance. Getting lost was always an underlying fear, but hats off to the Pinhoti trail marker dudes. The trail was well-marked, and we had no issues. Others did.

We started the climb to the Pinnacle. By our standards, it was no Pigeon Hill or Becky's Bluff, but it was an Alpe D'huez–style climb, switching back and forth. That wasn't bad either. The worst part was we could see the lights from the aid station, even hear their voices, but it still took a half hour to get there. Even at mile 74, climbing steep mountains, Rami was hiking fast and not worried about the hill. What he hated most was hearing and seeing the aid station and going out away from it several times in switchbacks that took it out of sight.

All Rami talked about before the race was the cheese egg sandwiches at this aid station supported by the GUTS crew. We got there, and he wanted nothing to do with it. Soup, Heed, M&Ms, refill water, thank the crew for being in the middle of nowhere, and head out. Walking out of the aid station, Rami decided that walking/hiking as fast as we could would be the order of the day. Running hurt his feet too much and gave too much chance for further injury. Walking was better for his stomach too. Anytime he ate, he was nauseous for about fifteen minutes. So getting him to eat was like feeding a toddler sometimes. To his credit, he knew his feeding schedule, but every time he ate, he felt bad for fifteen minutes, so he didn't want to. As we moved along in silence, Rami said, "You are the perfect guy for this. You don't have much to say." I asked if Bob and Rob had much to say, and he said, "Not really. They just talk a lot." I took it as a compliment. My concentration on salt, direction, food, pace math, and well, my own salt, hydration, and fuel kept me plenty busy.

Now, walking down this fire road that we knew lasted a couple miles, the anti-Rami shows up. The off-road runner loved this road. A new worry cropped up. When do we hit single track again? Also, the pace math starts in earnest. I did calculations for him no less than fifty to sixty times over the next seven hours. Leaving Pinnacle at 1:00 a.m., we were three hours ahead of cutoff pace. Rami became curious about current pace as well. Fortunately, I love this stuff too. I set up my Garmin to keep current pace, pace between each aid station, and overall pace available at all times. We also noticed that we were in no-man's-land. The twenty-four-hour-pace guys were well ahead, and the truly struggling were well behind. We went at least three hours without seeing one runner.

To be honest, due to sleep deprivation and the monotony of only seeing as far as your headlamp, I couldn't tell you much about the next 11 miles. The highlights? Fire road, good; single track, bad. I took the lead for a while because Rami wanted to follow feet and not have me yelling, "Left, left, left, or right, right, right," as he'd wander off in the woods. Then there was the first runner to come from behind and pass us was on a ridge running section right before an aid station. Some poor mountain bikers had set up camp about two hundred yards before the aid station, not knowing what was about to happen to them. We got to the station at 2:25 a.m. We'd actually banked time! Rami, while an impressive man to start, became even more impressive. He was a machine. We were moving sub eighteen-minute pace in some nasty, hard-to-negotiate, single track. We filled up with water. None of the food was appealing, and without G2 from the crew, Rami accepted Heed in his handheld. We went along the ridge line on a fire road for 4 miles, which was awesome because that only left 2.5 miles of single track to the next aid station.

Bulls Gap. It is funny how your world collapses to just a few things in a situation like this. You watch out for your runner, stay fueled, and follow the trail to the next aid station. The aid workers seemed foreign. Scott appeared next to us as if out of nowhere. We got G2, dropped long sleeve shirts, and hit the road. Ten more miles until we saw Scott again. At the time, we didn't know it, but the worst trails were behind us. We headed down the fire road, and Rami was curious how long it lasted. I didn't ask the aid station worker how long, but I said about four miles. Thankfully, I was correct!

Rocky Mount Church. An aid station at an intersection set up in the middle of the road told me were really out in the boonies, but it was a road, and Rami was happy with that. During the night, I lost my appetite as well—Liquid and gel, good; solid, bad. Rami would drink the broth and throw away the noodles. Eleven miles left in this puppy, and to be honest, my fear of me finishing was gone. I was worried about 32 miles, but my fitness was there, and my feet hurt, but I was not stopping because I saw the strength and will in Rami to finish this. There was absolutely no way this was not a done deal. There was only 5.58 miles to Scott and the Watershed stop, but most of all, there was daylight! The dark was getting to us both. Not counting me handing Rami his bottle and saying, "Drink this" or "Eat a gel" or "You can take salt" or "Give me the TRISLIDE." We spoke mostly about pace and time to home. We had several short discussions. One that stuck with me was Rami said he could never be a navy SEAL because of the sleep deprivation of hell week. As I drove home, knowing that he'd been up for close to thirty hours and covered 100 miles in less than twenty-seven hours, I thought he could absolutely be a navy SEAL. I've never heard of a navy SEAL doing this as part of his training.

Watershed felt like it was ten hours away. Time had slowed. Tenths of miles came slowly and painfully in our mind, and yet our pace was still awesome. We kept moving, and that is all we needed to do at this point. We got to the aid station and started the process that we'd perfected by then—Find water, fill the handheld, find soup, and *poof!* Scott was standing there. He did it again. Actually, I saw him as we came up, but it really didn't register. It was daylight now! We ditched headlights. I was so happy about that. Everyone else was on their way to the stop to see us, but we were done, and the focus was laser-like on the finish. We bolted. We actually went past Rob's truck, with him lying in the back of it, and didn't even see it. We did ask a runner how much single track was left since he had done this race before, and he lied. He said, "Fire road or paved road from here on out." We encountered a trail that was essentially a flood washout downhill, and we both wanted to punch the *liar*.

For the longest time, we heard cows mooing very loudly. Rami said if I wasn't with him, he'd actually be scared. I told him a joke about a bull, and he laughed for a split second. He said that he would laugh more but didn't have the energy. We crossed fields, dams, and more fields and dams. All the sudden, Vickie appeared from behind. She was itching to run. She was training for a fifty miler on Catalina Island. She ran next to us for a while and said many, many words in a very cheerful and happy tone, but it was bothersome. Right when Rami was going to tell her to go away, she said, "You want me to stay or go?" She left.

We made it to the paved road. The anti-Rami was very happy. He was now walking at about a fifteen-minute pace. I would fall off the pace because I couldn't walk that fast, and I'd run ahead and start walking. After doing that a couple times, Rami said, "You can't goad me into running." I laughed. I said, "I can't walk as fast as you. I'm just doing my best to keep up." Support started showing up about 1.5 miles out, Vickie and Ryan (Rami's son) appeared, then Ben (Bob's son), then Hana (Rami's daughter), Rhonda (Bob's wife), Bob, and Scott. We can see the stadium. Rami said that he was going to cry, and I was already trying not to. I was so happy for Rami. A hundred miler became much more of an impressive feat than I've ever considered it to be, now that I've experienced it firsthand. We see Rami's wife and Rob S. in the stands. One thing we didn't know, but our orange Team Rami shirts created a bond that all other runners and crews recognized. We later learned that other runners and crew would tell our crew where we were. Coming into aid stations, they'd say, "Your guys are right behind me."

The finish!

My job as pacer is done! My job as lifelong friend starts. I must never let him do this again.

Rami said, "Thank you, Troy. You have *no* idea how much your time with me helped me out! You are a true friend forever!"

Back to Rami write-up…

## *Miles 95–100.59*

During the long night, my friend Scott H. offered to make it to every aid station that family and crew could not. He was another wonderful friend who sacrificed a weekend for me. I cannot thank him enough. My family made it to around midnight and then headed back to the hotel to try to get some sleep before coming back for the finish.

After I picked up Troy, Scott came to a few aid stations with cold drinks and supplies in case I needed them. I felt so bad for him, staying up all night, and all I cared about or needed was cold G2. It was wonderful to see a friend at the aid stations, however, so I am really glad he made it through the night.

Only a person who has done one of these races can understand how much motivation and uplift a five-minute visit with a friend of family member can do for you.

Thank you, Scott H.

At the mile 95 aid station, I wanted in and out as fast as possible; at this point, only a broken leg or kidney dropping out of my body would stop me. I tried to wolf down some soup, filled up the water bottle, and told Scott I would see him at the finish!

We were told it was fire road and regular road all the way to the finish, which was wrong.

It hurt, but I didn't care. I was going to finish.

About 4 miles out, my wife's friend, Vikki, comes running up to run with us. She is a wonderful person, and I feel honored and blessed that she traveled from California to help crew my race.

However, she is very talkative and very upbeat, which I love normally, but this was too far from the finish to start "happy talk." Four miles could still take me ninety minutes if I started slowing down! Just when I was about to ask her to run ahead, she asked, "Should I just run ahead?"

Worked out perfectly. Thank you for not taking anything personally, Vikki!

With about 1.5 miles to go, we got out onto a road and started a long, straight path to the finish. At this point, I was still not running, but I was walking so fast that Troy had to drop back and run past me 'cause he couldn't keep up with my fifteen-minute-per-mile walking pace!

Then my son Ryan and Vikki showed up to run the final miles with us. I was fine with it now. I was still being a dad, even after being awake, moving, and on my feet for almost twenty-seven hours, and I kept yelling at Ryan to stay off the road!

Then Ben T., son of my friend Bob "Bubbala," showed up to run with us. Then I could see everyone at the turn to the stadium, and I knew we were almost home.

At this point, I started to get really emotional. I'd told my family that I might cry a lot at the end and that they should be ready. Once I could see the stadium, I pushed myself to start running and ran the quarter mile around the track with my whole family and crew to cross the finish line!

Twenty-six hours, fifty-two minutes—that's three hours and eight minutes ahead of the cutoffs. I had given back virtually nothing of the time I had gained in the first fifty miles.

# IMMEDIATELY POSTRACE

*I have fought the good fight, I have finished the race, I have kept the faith.*

—2 Timothy 4:7 (NIV)

I cannot tell you how happy I was! I screamed out, "We raised almost $9,000 for the night shelter!"

Everyone is happy, everyone is congratulating me, and Scott H. comes up and pledges $500 to put us solidly over $9,000!

And I finally, after almost twenty-seven hours, sit down.

What a feeling.

Then I take off my shoes.

Wow, I knew I had some pain, but this was ugly. I had blisters on top of my blisters. My feet were so swollen that they looked like hobbit feet.

Had a cold Coke and stared at the wonderful belt buckle I had just suffered for.

Would have stayed there for a long time soaking it all in, but it was cold and starting to rain, so we all started to pack it in.

Getting up out of that chair was almost as hard as the race!

I hobbled to the car, and we drove back to the hotel.

Another God moment was that Heather was never able to make it to my car, which I left at the start; it had my change of clothes in it. This was not a problem because since the weather never got cold, I had warm clothes from my aid station number 4 bag ready to go!

I took off my clothes to get in the shower and looked at myself in the mirror. The rash will not be described here, but suffice it to say, it was one of the most painful showers I have ever taken. Bob's wife actually had some prescription-strength topical cream to help with rash that was another godsend.

## The Ride Home and Day After

We got in the car to drive home. It was kind of a blur because I was trying to sleep, but what I do remember is this.

- I remember enjoying two Egg McMuffins and hash browns.

- I remember walking to the bathroom in McDonalds and feeling like I was a hundred years old. The step outside the restaurant felt like it was twelve feet high. I actually stood in front of it for about thirty seconds, contemplating how I could climb up it. It was about three inches high.

- A little boy offered to help me up the step; he probably thought I was handicapped. It really was super funny.

- Every time I fell asleep, my legs would start "running" and wake me up.

- I was very, very edgy and kept telling Heather to be careful and slow down!

We got home and ordered pizza. We had someone from church come over and bring communion and do some prayers with us, which was so nice. I cannot imagine getting through an hour of mass, much less kneeling and standing up and sitting down!

I made it till 6:00 p.m. and then slept solid until 7:00 a.m. Monday.

## *The Day after the Day After*

On Monday, I woke up more sore, mostly in my feet, than I have ever been in my life. Interestingly, my quads and hamstrings were not that bad. Everything from my knees down (knees were doing fantastic also) was just completely shot and inflamed.

I was able to get around the house using crutches and with help from the kids and Heather.

Heather said that Monday was basically like taking care of someone after an operation.

I spent most of the day in bed, eating (I was finally hungry; breakfast was two eggs, two bagels with cream cheese and lox, and orange juice, followed by mint chocolate chip ice cream a few hours later), staying caught up on Facebook with how everyone I knew finished and how they were feeling, and starting to write about my experience.

As I wrote this, it was only about forty-eight hours after my finish.

My overwhelming feeling was happiness and appreciation that God let me finish this amazing feat.

I was also very reluctant to reenter into the real world.

The world I have lived in for the days leading up to the race, during the race especially, and immediately postrace was amazing and *so* rare for an adult.

Every need I had was taken care of by people I loved.

No one could possibly be offended if I said or did something wrong.

I was getting kudos constantly.

Who would want to leave this world?

So I have decided I won't.

I don't mean I will not go back to work or stop being a responsible parent, husband, or person.

I mean that this race had changed me on a very deep level. I don't know if it will last, I pray that it does, but I am a different person today than I was on Saturday morning, November 3.

I am so appreciative for the family and friends who helped me. I cannot imagine how people do this alone.

# PART 4
# SUMMING IT UP

*I have not achieved it, but I focus on this one thing:*
*Forgetting the past and looking forward to what*
*lies ahead, I press on to reach the end of the race and*
*receive the heavenly prize.*

—Philippians 3:13 (NLT)

# OKAY, WHAT HAVE I LEARNED?

*All Scripture is breathed out by God and profitable for teaching, for reproof, for correction, and for training in righteousness.*

—2 Timothy 3:16 (ESV)

As I write this, it was exactly a week after finishing Pinhoti. My overwhelming feeling this week was *peacefulness.* Truly, it's a peacefulness that I had not had for a long, long time.

If ever.

I kept waiting for the feeling to wear off, but I was starting to think that completing this race really did change me on a very basic, deep level.

I really prayed that it would last because I really liked the new Rami.

And from some comments from friends and coworkers, I think others do to!

I think that completing something that challenges you on this level—and this really did challenge me, almost more than I can articulate—spills over into the very core of who you are.

The week after, the things that normally bother me just don't as much. I was accepting God's will much more than I ever had.

Trust me, the week after the race was not perfect or without trials and tribulations.

They just didn't seem to matter as much.

For example, for weeks up until the race, my wife and I were not getting along, and I was very angry at her.

The week after, I was not angry and could not even remember why I had been angry!

Maybe this could be a new form of marriage therapy.

All you have to do is train and plan for about thirty years for a hundred-mile race, complete it without dying, and all your problems will not seem as important anymore.

Wonder how many patients I would have?

I was not as rushed. I was spending more time talking to people when I would normally move on to something "important" that I was working on. I was appreciating my life, family, work, etc. much more than on November 2!

I had a ton of challenges in my life from 2008 to 2013.

This race taught me what is or was truly important and, more importantly, where to put my energy and focus.

I will do my best now to draw some correlations to finishing a hundred-mile off-road running race in under thirty hours and dealing with the challenges we face in this wonderful thing we call life!

## Why?

I am sure it will come as no shock whatsoever that I get asked why on a very regular basis!

Ever since I started doing things that were not the norm, I have had to answer this question many times, whether it was racing motocross instead of playing baseball, or running before class in college after getting two hours sleep, or training for my first triathlon, first marathon, first Ironman, or first ultra.

*Why* was a common conversation starter and, often, finisher.

You know what, after fifty years on this earth, it is still not easy to answer. Funny thing is, the people who would really understand your answer are the ones that are doing it with you. So, of course, they never ask.

They already know why.

One of my favorite answers came from Mark Allen, arguably one of the best short- and long-course triathletes of all time. "It is a finish line you have to cross to understand." This is very, very true. Trying to explain to someone who has never run or thinks running one mile is agony why you are training for an ultramarathon can be quite frustrating. For both parties!

So I thought about it a bit and jotted down a few reasons I have heard others say that resonate with me.

1. It is a finish line you have to cross to understand.

2. If you have to ask the question, you really would never understand the answer.

To expound on this, here's a bit from a personal viewpoint.

1. Because I can.

2. Because I am blessed to be able to.

3. Because I feel really alive when I do.

4. Because I really, really like it.

5. Because it brings me closer to God.

6. Because I pray more often,

7. better,

8. and longer during and after.

9. Because it makes me a better father,

10. friend,

11. husband,

12. and business owner.

13. Because it calms me down.

14. Because it excites me.

15. Because it challenges me and helps me find my limits.

16. Because I am competitive and want to see how well I can do (not much of a why lately but used to be).

17. Because I want to stay young at heart.

18. Because I enjoy nature.

19. Because I can do it with my family.

20. Because my social life revolves around it.

21. Because it is one of the only things that makes me feel raw.

22. Because others don't do it. I like being different.

23. Because others do it. I like being around like-minded people.

24. Because it gives me purpose.

25. Because I can.

So that gives you a small idea of the why. The best way to truly answer this question is to join me on a trail run. Almost everyone (almost—some still think I am nuts after trying it) who goes out on a trail run starts to understand a bit of why I love it so much.

## *How?*

The next most common question I get is how.

I will be completely honest. Sometimes, well, most of the time, I really don't know how I do and did this.

I will share with you what worked for me and, more importantly, how this might become a blueprint for any very large, scary, and worthwhile goal you might have in your life.

There are many ways to get to the start and finish line of an ultramarathon. In fact, I would venture to guess that of the 240 people who signed up (BTW, if you like statistics, 192 actually started (a 20 percent DNS rate), 107 finished (a 44 percent DNF rate), and I was fifty-fourth overall, almost exactly in the middle of the finishers—not that any of that really matters), there were 240 different plans on how to approach this race.

I am not a natural runner. I am not a natural at anything athletic, except maybe racquetball, bowling, and billiards. I am larger by many, many pounds than your average ultrarunner. I run about 50 percent of the volume that I see most of my ultrarunning friends doing. I did not play any competitive sports as a child, except for two years of Little League baseball and fourteen years of racing motocross.

For some reason, I am able to finish events that, for the most part, I should not be able to. This is not bragging. It is really just my honest assessment of where I am as an athlete.

As I look back and connect the dots—as Steve Jobs so eloquently put it before his untimely death—I find some things that I think might have helped me finish and might help you, the reader, finish whatever ultra you are attempting in life.

## *Commit and Be Accountable.*

I do best when I have concrete and measurable goals. I also do best under pressure as proven by my picking a goal like the 100 miler that was really outside my box. I didn't tell a lot of people this before my race, but I was more frightened about this race than I had ever been before. I was nervous before other races, but for most of them, I had either completed the actual distance in training or a huge percent of the distance.

Before this race, my longest run was just over 50 percent of the race distance, and about 44 percent of the longest previous *time* I had run.

Think of that for a minute. It is kind of like training for a marathon and stopping when your long run reaches ten to thirteen miles.

Multiplied by four.

Or, an ever better comparison, if your marathon took you four hours to complete, the longest time you ran at any one time in training was one hour and forty-five minutes.

Who does that?

So, to put it mildly, this was a big "stretch" goal.

This kept me focused on the prize, which was crossing that finish line in under thirty hours.

Once I signed up (for the second time) for this race, I designed a plan and committed to completing as much training as my body, mind, spirit, and life circumstances could possibly allow/handle.

For the most part, I stuck to this commitment.

I also made myself more accountable to more people for this race than I had ever done before. I am a person that tends to tell a lot of people about his goals, and this was the mack daddy in my book.

I told all my friends. I told everyone I knew at church and asked for prayers from everyone I knew who was religious. I told and e-mailed, repeatedly, everyone on our e-mail list at work. I talked about it on social media incessantly. I used this race to raise money for a good cause, and this allowed me to reach out to our whole church to ask for donations. I convinced three friends to train with me to be my pacers. I convinced family and friends to be there the whole weekend.

With all this on the line, plus my own internal drive to finish what I start, I left myself with no options.

## *Leave No Options*

One of the things I heard many times from people leading up to this race was, "I am going to do my best, but if it isn't in the cards, I will just pull out and sign up for another 100 miler."

This was not an option for me.

I think this might have been the true driving force to get me through the training and the race.

It bears mentioning here that getting through the training and to the start line uninjured and ready to race is an ultra in itself. There were 240 people who signed up, and only 192 actually started (20 percent DNS or did not start rate). There were also a ton of people who did show up to the start but were definitely not at 100 percent due to various injuries, sicknesses, etc. Not the way you want to begin a thirty-hour running journey.

I went into this race with a do-or-die mentality. Not really die, but in my mind, they would have to pull me off this course for medical reasons or because I was behind the time cutoffs before I would DNF.

This was a *huge* sacrifice for me and my family, and I did not want to feel that I had to do it again.

So I went in, truly with no options.

I think this is how we should approach everything in our lives that means something to us—staying married, being an engaged and loving parent, keeping your business moving forward and alive in hard times, staying committed to your religious life, and staying true to your values, morals, and goals in life.

I think that in today's society, we attempt great things, such as a lifelong marriage, but do not put a great effort or drive into them. I cannot tell you how many people I talk to that say, "I'll get married, but if it gets tough, I will just get a separation or divorce."

No options.

I went into this race with a singular focus. I would rather sacrifice my time, sleep, etc. for a one-time amazing goal than commit only partially with the thought of "if it gets too hard, I will just pull out and do another race."

I arrived at the start line as close to 100 percent as a person could be. Interestingly, most of the nagging injuries I had during training did not bother me at all during the race. This I attributed to two things—the almost unbearable amount of pain in my feet that suppressed all other pain and, more importantly, the incredible number of people praying for me.

## *The Basics*

I won't spend a lot of time on this as there are plenty of people out there who know way more than I do about this side of the sport. I will say, however, that putting in the long miles is 100 percent necessary (i.e., the people who think they can finish one of these without doing any endurance running). In addition, I feel that consistent weight training and core work, even during the peak of the run training, is 100 percent necessary also.

It becomes very clear, after you obtain a certain level of aerobic conditioning, that this race is more about muscular strength and mental focus than it is about your VO2 max or lactate threshold (at least for us just-wanna-finish athletes). I cannot imagine getting to this start line uninjured and strong enough to finish without the consistent (two to three sessions per week) strength training, functional, and traditional weight training workouts I did. I am sure there are people who can get away with just running, but I feel they are few and far between.

Just my humble opinion. And it is not influenced by the fact that I own a fitness club, at all.

Really.

## *Prayer: By Me and for Me*

I believe strongly that this, by far, was the determining factor in my finishing this race. I cannot count how many people were doing rosaries, praying silently, praying in groups before, during, and after the run, etc.

My faith that prayer works was never more evident than on November 3 to 4 of 2012. I could literally feel the uplift that comes with a prayer coming my way, and I know that during my downtimes, the prayers helped me to trust that things would get better and better, not worse.

I felt God with me from the minute I woke up (at 2:30 a.m. on Saturday, BTW) till I crossed the finish line at 8:52 a.m. on Sunday!

Prayer works, period.

## *Do Something You Love as a BHAG*

At my first ultra, I got to hear David Horton (an ultrarunning stud, for sure) speak about BHAGs. What is a BHAG, you ask?

> Big
> Hairy
> Audacious
> Goal

He, of course, was talking about ultrarunning at levels I will never see (never say never, I know; maybe when I am retired and kids are out of the house) like running across the United States or running the whole Appalachian Trail.

But his point was well-taken, and it was about having goals that scare you, put you outside of your box, challenge you, and have a pretty high chance of failure.

In my book, these are the goals that are worth fighting for.

In order to achieve a BHAG, I feel you can stack the deck by making it something you love to do to start.

By now, it is no secret that I *love* trail running. It is really one of my favorite things to do.

This being said, this was a *huge* amount of running for me, in training and in the race, to achieve this goal. Even with my love of running, there were times, more than once, that I wanted to quit a training session.

I also love alone time and being alone on the trails.

Again, there were many times, especially when I was training tired and the training runs got over four hours, that I craved some human contact and conversation.

The point here is, if you want to do something epic, as we are so fond of saying in the endurance sports world, start with an activity you truly love.

Because even if you love it, the amount of time needed to achieve a BHAG will tax your love for *any* activity, trust me! Even chocolate ice cream can make you sick if you eat enough of it. I think.

It won't be easy, for sure.

But it will be a heck of a lot easier than if you pick something that you only marginally like or, deep down, don't like at all.

## *Team Effort*

Ultrarunning and running in general is, at its core, a solo endeavor.

You are relying on yourself, your physical strength, your mental toughness, and your spirit to finish each workout and race.

This is one of the reasons I love it so much.

However, this event was really all about my team.

First of all, my family and friends supported (for the most part) what I was planning to do. This helps a ton, as I know others who love this sport but struggle with a nonsupportive spouse and/or family.

I cannot imagine how hard that is.

I took a team of ten people with me to Alabama that weekend—my family, crew, and pacers. They were all there to support me, and I cannot thank them enough for their time and sacrifice to help get me to the line.

My wife and I decided it would be best for me to go the night before by myself. I was pretty darn nervous and would be trying to get to bed by 7:30  p.m., not a good recipe to bring family and friends along.

This was a great decision and worked out perfectly.

We also decided, due to the logistics of following a point-to-point race and getting to all the aid stations, that the first time I would see them would be at the mile 41 aid station, which is about nine to ten hours into the race and on top of the highest mountain in Alabama.

This was another great decision. My low point of the race was actually from mile 27–35 (due to heat and stomach issues, which, BTW, continued to plague me for the rest of the race). Knowing that I would see my whole family and friends at mile 41 kept me going and really was the highlight of the race for me.

Except for the finish, of course.

My team motivated me with hugs, cheers, and really cute and funny signs. We all wore the same shirts that promoted the homeless shelter we were raising money for. My pacers were fantastic and kept me company and alive during the really low times during the night.

I don't know if I would have finished without them, and if I did, it would not have been nearly so sweet.

You might think you can achieve BHAGs alone, but I am here to tell you that you really cannot.

## *Make It Not Only about You!*

Training for and completing a hundred-mile ultramarathon is a very selfish thing to do. Anyone who tells you it is not is not being truthful with you or themselves.

When I decided to fully commit to this goal, I did not want it to be a *completely* selfish act. I wanted to give the glory and thanks to God that I could even attempt this and give something to those in need.

So I decided to make this run a fund-raising event.

Months before the start, I met with the head of our church (who, BTW, was also part of my team, as he drove two hours to the start to give me a blessing before I headed out—amazing) to decide which charity to raise money for. Pretty quickly, we both decided we wanted to do something local. Large charities are wonderful, but a lot of the money you raise goes to administrative costs. We wanted every penny to go to those who needed it!

We decided on the night shelter, a homeless shelter for men in downtown Atlanta.

I am involved with this shelter through the men's club at my church. We go down there twice a year to feed the men and spend the night with them. It is really an eye-opening experience, and trust me, you will have a tough time complaining about your life or circumstances after you spend time down there.

Anyway, I also decided to have people sponsor me per mile, instead of a flat donation. This was a partly selfish act, as I knew it would help motivate me to keep pushing on, as each mile would be more money for the men in need!

Making this race not all about me was a wonderful decision and helped my training and my motivation to finish.

As of this writing, we were actually inching up toward $100 per mile (my original goal was $30 per mile)!

I did my best to run for God, and God rewarded me by allowing me to finish.

Postscript: we raised just over $10,000—the largest one-time donation in the history of the shelter (open over thirty years). The director of the shelter actually told me that this donation was equal to 25 percent of their yearly operating budget!

Praise God!

## *How Did I Feel After?*

Peaceful, complete, blessed, and thankful.

I am so thankful that God allowed me to start and finish this race. I cannot imagine how people in my situation (those looking to do this just once) felt the day after if they DNFed.

This race changed me on a very deep level, in ways I cannot truly articulate yet. More on that later, but know that the changes are all positive and amazing. Just ask my family and friends!

## *What Is Next?*

"What's next?"

This is probably the fourth most common question I get after why, how, and "How bad did it hurt?" or "What were your high and low points?"

I am not surprised when people ask this question. After all, those that know me well know that in 2008, I did my first off-road run—a 10K that took me fifty-one minutes—and slowly increased my training and racing distances up to a forty miler in 2009, a fifty-three miler in 2010 and a hundred miler in 2012!

The common assumption is that I would attempt 120 miles, or 150, or 200 miles in my near future.

So what is next?

Honestly, I don't know and, really, I am not thinking too much about it right now.

I will tell you this, unless something drastically changed in my life (like winning the lottery, which I don't ever play), I will not train and do another race of this distance again.

I am so committed to this statement that I told my final pacer, Troy B. that his job did not end after running with me for 32 miles and ten hours. His job—to make sure I don't sign up for another one of these when the pain and agony wore off—was just beginning!

I also had my wife film me at the end, with my good friend, who is an attorney, present, saying I will never do this again.

I am serious about this.

It is not the pain I felt during the race, although it was beyond anything I have ever felt at times.

It is the sacrifices I needed to make to get to the start line.

Even though I trained much less than most of my friends, I still committed a huge amount of my weekly free time to running, traveling to running places, prepping for runs, recovery from runs, eating for runs, etc.

As mentioned, I absolutely love trail running, and this experience was amazing and life-changing, really.

But, for now, it was a bucket list item to be checked off.

A one and done.

I know I am serious about this because I did it with my Ironman race. One was more than enough for me.

Many people asked me—and I know even more thought it but didn't verbalize it—"Do you think this level of running is healthy?"

Here is my answer. I really think we are meant to run long distances, specifically in nature (not on roads). I think that if you have the time to commit to this lifestyle in a balanced, healthy way (i.e., keeping the volume of running appropriate for your body, great nutrition, low stress, eight to ten hours of quality sleep per night, etc.) that this is a *very* healthy way to live.

That being said, an almost fifty-year-old married man who has two young children and is running a small business cannot possibly approach this in a healthy level.

Unless he sacrifices something important in another area of his life.

I was more than willing to sacrifice for four to six months to achieve this goal, and I have absolutely no regrets that I did.

I will not continue to sacrifice to do another. I have other things I want to do with my life.

Please don't get me wrong. I completely understand the addiction and pull to do more than one of these races. And I would be lying if I told you that, after the pain subsided a bit, I didn't start second-guessing my race performance.

But this pull is nothing compared to the pull of my family, my religious journey, and my career.

This does not mean, of course, that I will quit trail running.

I will take some time to think about what appeals to me and shoot for that goal!

Right now, I am thinking of taking up golf or joining a bowling league.

Thank you all for joining me on this journey. The journey never ends. It will now just change—to what, I have no idea, and I am okay and happy with that.

God bless you all!

# Appendix A

## *Exercise and Spirituality*

### *Psychological Benefits*

- Self-esteem
- Self-confidence
- Reduces stress
- Reduces anxiety
- Increases our overall vibrancy and energy
- Natural antidepressant

### *Spiritual Benefits*

- It improves the mind-body connection (healthy body = healthy mind).
- Our bodies were meant to move, be part of nature.
- The improvement of oxygen delivery to the brain helps to clear the mind.
- High intensity brings us to a raw place and gets us more in touch with inner self and closer to God; it clears your mind of noise.
- It is a form of meditation in movement.
- Its calming effect allows clear thoughts to emerge.
- You have improved creativity.

- Allowing your mind to wander, especially in nature, allows you to see the world from a new perspective.

- There is an increase in your sense of connectedness.

- You get or improve the ability to contemplate deeper values and meditate.

- Exercising outdoors allows us to appreciate God's beauty and the wonderment of being alive.

- It sets a good example for your family; take care of yourself before you can take care of others!

- It increases your feeling of community.

- Social interaction with other like-minded, healthy adults

- It improves your spiritual routine (doing something daily).

- You get or improve goal-attainment efficacy (achieve exercise goals, achieve spiritual goals).

- It increases our sense of adventure/belief we can do anything (i.e., like a child)

- It increases our compassion for others.

- It stills the noisiness of life and gives you peace.

- BE IN MOMENT MORE WITH PRAYER – TRANSFER OVER TO OTHER AREAS OF LIFE!

# Appendix B

## *How Do We Do This? How Do We Attain the Level Needed for These Benefits?*

### *Long-Term Goals: Exercise Plan*

It will take each individual a different amount of time to reach these goals based on exercise history, medical conditions, compliance to the program, etc.

#### *Cardiovascular*

- Three to five days per week (depending on goals and intensity)
- Ten to sixty minutes per session (Two hundred-plus minutes average per week for weight loss)
- Done *after* your weight training or first thing in the morning, when it's most effective
- Variety in intensity and type of exercise (this helps you reach goals quicker)
- Heart rate (get a monitor)—60 percent to 80 percent of max (220-age)

#### *Weight (Strength) Training*

- Two to five days per week
- Thirty to forty-five minutes per session

- Variety, intensity, and consistency are key!

### *Flexibility*

- Do mobility work *before* you exercise.
- Stretch during and *after* you exercise (make sure you are warm).
- Do three to five minutes minimum; the longer the better.
- Hold each stretch for twenty to thirty seconds.
- No bouncing! No pain!

### *A Great Week of Exercise (Long-Term Goal)*

Mon:10-minute cardiovascular warm-up

30–45 minutes weight training

10–30 minutes of cardio

Stretch!

Tues:30–60 minutes of cardio

Stretch!

Wed:10-minute cardiovascular warm-up

30–45 minutes of weight training

10–30 minutes of cardio

Stretch!

Thurs:30–60 minutes of cardio

Stretch!

Fri:10-minute cardiovascular warm-up

30–45 minutes of weight training

10–30 minutes of cardio

Stretch!

Sat:30–90 minutes very easy cardio or recreational exercise / stretch!

Sun:Day off or recreational exercise for the Lord (play and pray!)

## *Attitude*

The longer I live, the more I realize the impact of attitude on life. Attitude, to me, is more important than facts. It is more important that the past, than education, than money, than circumstances, than failures, than successes, than what other people think or say or do. It is more important than appearance, giftedness, or skill. It will make or break a company... a church... a home. The remarkable thing is we have a choice every day regarding the attitude we will embrace for that day. We cannot change our past...we cannot change the fact that people will act in a certain way. We cannot change the inevitable. The only thing we can do is play on the one string that we have, and that is our attitude... I am convinced that life is 10 percent what happens to me and 90 percent how I react to it. And so it is with you... we are in charge of our attitudes.

—Charles Swindoll

Choice, not chance, determines your destiny.

—Aristotle

Made in the USA
Columbia, SC
16 April 2025

56730803R00115